Community Power Structure

. Propositional Inventory, Tests, and Theory

Claire W. Gilbert

University of Florida Press / Gainesville / 1972

───────────────────────────

Library of Congress Cataloging in Publication Data

Gilbert, Claire W   1928–
    Community power structure.
    (University of Florida social sciences monograph
no. 45)
    Includes bibliographical references.
    1. Community power. 2. Municipal government—
United States. 3. Political participation—United
States. I. Title. II. Series: Florida.
University, Gainesville. University of Florida
monographs. Social sciences, no. 45
JS331.G55   329   78–189818
ISBN 0–8130–0356–3

───────────────────────────

SERIES DESIGNED BY STANLEY D. HARRIS

MANUFACTURED BY THE
ROSE PRINTING COMPANY
TALLAHASSEE, FLORIDA

Acknowledgments

Research was supported by the International City Managers' Association and the National Science Foundation.

I should like to acknowledge the help of my colleague at Hunter College of the City University of New York, Lindsey Churchill, with whom I consulted on the final manuscript. The research from which this monograph developed was conducted while the author was associated with Northwestern University. Scott Greer of that institution will recognize some of his ideas put to use. Finally, I particularly want to thank Douglas M. Fox of the University of Connecticut, without whom this manuscript would not have gotten into print.

Thanks must go also to the Graduate School of the University of Florida for making possible the publication of this monograph.

Contents

1. Community Power Literature and Its Use in Secondary
   Analysis   1

2. Community Power: Empirical Generalizations   6

3. The Development of Community Power Theory   59

1. Community Power Literature and Its Use in Secondary Analysis

THIS STUDY is based upon the assumption that through a systematic inventory of existing knowledge of community power, we can evaluate generalizations and hypotheses and test them with gathered data, thus contributing to the building of more sophisticated theory. Community power structure is used here as a blanket concept referring to related phenomena of political process, decision-making on the local level, and so forth; no assumption is made about the stability or integration of any structure. The current work is considered important because for more than a decade, scholars have been unable to agree on interpretations of existing research, methodology, and theory in the field of community power.

Although there has been an interest in local politics and community power for decades, social science was greatly stimulated by Floyd Hunter's publication in 1954 of *Community Power Structure*. Hunter, using a sociological orientation, was innovative in his methodology. His work was widely reviewed in sociological, political science, and administrative science journals.[1] He received a great amount of praise, but was also the subject of sharp criticism, particularly with regard to his assumption that a power structure exists, his innovative methodology (which some critics believe was the *source* of his findings), and his conclusion that a power elite existed in "Regional City."

In retrospect, we can see that the pluralist-oriented political scientists were irritated and stimulated by the community power research of sociologists, and they increased greatly their quantity

1. (Chapel Hill: University of North Carolina Press). One review of the literature is C. W. Gilbert, "The Study of Community Power Studies," in Scott Greer et al., eds., *The New Urbanization* (New York: St. Martin's Press, 1968), pp. 222–45.

1

of research into local community politics. They questioned the validity of the findings of many elite- or stratification-oriented sociologists. They tried to show that their work was more valid, using methods of criticism and empirical research. Their findings indicated more diffusion of power in local communities than some sociologists had found. Sociologists continued with their studies of community power in the late 1950s and 1960s. Some incorporated the criticisms of the pluralists, others ignored them.

By the mid-1960s, a large number of community power studies were available. A large number of often contradictory theoretical orientations, hypotheses, generalizations, and findings were also available. The literature became ripe for codification. This work is an effort in that direction and it is hoped that this inventory will help to narrow the acceptable views.[2]

DATA QUALITY CONTROL

This inquiry is based on a secondary analysis of published empirical community power studies. An extensive job was done in reclassifying the description and data presented by these studies, in order to compare them and to make quantitative statements about the attributes of a variety of communities.

One may wonder how we can learn about communities with data derived from presumably biased sources. Raoul Naroll developed data quality control to deal with a similar problem. He used ethnographic reports to study culture stress. Like community power reports, those of ethnographers are not equally "trustworthy" or valid. Before his monograph appeared in 1962, the only systematic method of evaluating the trustworthiness of reports was the use of internal and external criticism developed by historians; Naroll offered a new method called data quality control.[3]

Data quality control deals with groups of reports compiled by a variety of inquirers under disparate conditions rather than with single reports. It is assumed that some records are made under

2. From a sociology of knowledge analysis, the finding emerged: despite the effects of bias and selectivity on the part of researchers, there still are objective conditions which force the variety in research findings. See C. W. Gilbert, "Communities, Power Structures, and Research Bias," *Polity* 4 (Winter 1971): 218–35.

3. *Data Quality Control—A New Research Technique* (Glencoe, Ill.: Free Press, 1962).

conditions of higher apparent trustworthiness than others. The data quality control method uses statistical reasoning, similar to that used in industrial production control: systematic comparison is made of data from reports made under "better" conditions with those made under "worse" conditions to see if they differ seriously. A difference (also called error, bias, or distortion) is considered serious when a data-factor (i.e., a dependent variable, such as participation of informals in the power structure) correlates with a control-factor (i.e., an extraneous variable, such as use of the reputational method) so strongly that its probability is due to chance less than three times in a thousand. Restated, a serious bias exists when a group of reports made under one condition differs three standard deviation units from a group of reports made under another condition, on their descriptions of a community power structure variable.

However, the effect of random bias on one or both variables in a correlation is almost always to reduce true correlations. When correlations are reduced as a result of bias, the null hypothesis is often supported when it should be rejected. Since the effect of one systematically distorted variable in a correlation is the lowering or obscuring of a true correlation, the effect of this kind of distortion does not create a correlation where none exists. An association only tends to be spuriously inflated when two variables in a correlation share an identical measurement error.[4] When two variables in a hypothesis share an identical measurement error, the control-factor can be held constant to see if the relationship of the hypothesis continues to hold.

Data quality control reasoning is applied in this work: community power studies are classified on a large number of factors which might be sources of bias. Seventy-three factors are examined for their biasing effects. They can be summarized as (1) characteristics of the researcher himself, (2) conceptual characteristics, (3) conditions of observation, (4) breadth of the study, (5) methods of reporting, and (6) work process.

Each measure of a dependent variable in a supported hypothesis is cross-classified with all quality control factors. If the data-factor is correlated beyond three sigmas ($P = 0.004$) with any of the control factors, then each measure of the independent variable is cross-classified and examined for association with the control

4. Ibid., chap. 1.

factor. Support for the hypothesis is not spurious if no association exists between the independent variable and the control factor. The results are thrown into question, however, if both measures are associated with the identical control factor.

PROCEDURES

Data were obtained for 166 cities[5] from secondary analyses of community power studies. Observations made by others were reclassified with respect to abstract or conceptual variables.[6]

The conditions under which the original description was created were also classified. Though rich description is reduced to simpler traits that can be more or less classified as either present or absent, an advantage is gained; many communities can be compared on a large number of characteristics, a comparison not possible when description is preserved in its original detail. The sample, development of the content analysis coding schedule, measures of concepts, interrelations of measures, estimates of validity, reliability, and replicability, appear elsewhere.[7]

Data are in nominal form. The research design seeks the presence or absence of traits, analyzing dichotomous variables in two-way classifications. Although many categories prove to be orderable, their orderability was not anticipated.

Probability values for tables are from Fisher's Exact Test of Probability, two-tailed, calculated by summing both tails of a distribution.[8] The level of alpha, rejection of the null hypothesis, is 0.15 (two-tailed), but the majority of coefficients presented are beyond 0.10.

THE VARIABLES[9]

In surveying the theoretical literature on community power, a pattern emerges which indicates, more or less clearly, two things: (1) which variables are objective and can be considered inde-

5. C. W. Gilbert, "The Study of Community Power Studies," and "Community Power Structure: A Study in the Sociology of Knowledge" (Ph.D. diss., Northwestern University, 1966), Appendix A.

6. Ibid., Appendix B.

7. Ibid., Appendixes A–C.

8. This follows Armsen's definition D–3 in P. Armsen, "Tables for Significance Tests of 2 x 2 Contingency Tables," *Biometrika* 42 (1955): 495–511. A discussion of this statistic is found in Arthur Banks and Robert Textor, *A Cross-Polity Survey* (Cambridge: M.I.T. Press, 1963), p. 29.

9. "Attribute" and "variable" are used interchangeably here.

pendent or underlying, and (2) which, though less objective (because data and agreement on data are harder to obtain), are often considered dependent or consequent variables, i.e., caused by the former.

1. The underlying variables are seen as three basic types. (A) Theorists such as Durkheim, C. W. Mills, and Shevky and Bell indicate that the temporal dimension is important because national changes are reflected in local communities. (B) Theorists like Wirth propose social variations between cities which differ in industrial makeup, location in a metropolitan region, age, national region, growth characteristics, size, density, and functional type. (C) Political science theorists tend to stress the importance of the local constitutional and political form, e.g., ward or at-large elections, partisan or nonpartisan, council or commission, manager system present or absent, and relative political homogeneity. Since most of these may be measured in a number of ways, there are sixty-six measures of independent variables.

2. The consequent variables (the structure of community power) have four conceptual dimensions. (A) The political organization involving party structures, councils, departments, elected and appointed officials, government employees, and experts. (B) The parapolitical organization[10] which includes business, newspaper, religious, educational, voluntary, and formal organizations and their leaders. (C) Informal organizations including ad hoc groups formed around particular issues. (D) Population of the city in terms of masses, minorities, economic classes, publics, and voters. Each of these dimensions may be examined to see which place they have in the formulation and execution of local public policy. There are fifty-nine measures of dependent variables.

Together, the underlying and consequent variables comprise the material from which community power theorists shape their models. Another factor, ideology, may be either an independent or dependent variable. With the exception of ideology,[11] all of these variables have been examined here.

10. Parapolitical refers to organizations which are not political in their primary function but can and often do perform political functions. See Scott Greer and Peter Orleans, "The Mass Society and the Parapolitical Structure," *American Sociological Review* 27 (October 1962): 634–46.

11. In retrospect I regret very much not having included ideology as one of the variables.

2. Community Power: Empirical Generalizations

In our search and coding of the community power literature, we extracted all of the empirically testable statements. These included hypotheses, generalizations, or suppositions. They are the substance of the propositional inventory, which is assembled to test its hypotheses with the gathered data.

All of the following independent variables are used in propositions inventoried and tested below: national trends, economic function and social characteristics of a community, population (size and growth), region of the country, city type, and constitutional structure. The interrelations of some dependent variables are also analyzed. All tables are analyzed for systematic biases (data quality controlled) and are considered "safe" unless otherwise noted.

It is appropriate to mention here that in another inquiry, I constructed an interrelated set of hypotheses based upon the economic functions of cities, their types (metropolitan, suburban, independent, farm, and so on), and their population sizes, in relation to power structures and participation. Limited applicability of the hypotheses is analyzed in terms of national structures, because much of our knowledge about local politics is based upon communities in the United States. Societal scale and national ideology (centralization and decentralization) are used as characteristics of nation-states within which disparate community characteristics (economic functions, formal political structures, and so on) make sense.[1] The characteristics of nation-states are discussed in chapter 3. The inventory is presented here with hypotheses grouped by their independent variables.

1. Gilbert, "Community Power Structure," pp. 30–34.

1. TRENDS

The independent variable here is time itself. Two related viewpoints provide a basis for predicting trends in community politics. First, the scale[2] of the United States is increasing, and we should expect to find greater interdependence and functional differentiation of local communities at a later rather than an earlier point in time.[3] Included in these changes are an increase in absentee ownership of local business firms and a trend toward national consolidation of corporations. Second, skills and attitudes of local populations are changing, a phenomenon which might result in their holding different expectations today about local government. All of the foregoing might be reflected in community power structures. The first set of hypotheses deals with such trends.

Trends and Power Structure

Before we proceed with the hypotheses, an operational explanation of "power structure" is offered. "Power structure" as a blanket concept includes all of the dependent variables of the study, such as degree of community conflict and the strength of politicians in the local community. However, "power structure" is also used in a different way when reference is made to a "ruling elite" or a "pluralistic power structure." So, although there are fifty-nine measures of power structure or dependent variables, nine of these deal with power structure in the special sense, i.e., as a general description of complicated processes, summarized by such terms as "pluralism" and "elitism." "Power structure" in the special sense refers to whatever degree of integration, or shape, that policy-making takes.

A common question is whether there is a ruling elite in the local community. Here, a community is coded as having a power elite only if there is a well-defined ruling group which dominates

2. Eshref Shevky and Wendell Bell, *Social Area Analysis* (Stanford: Stanford University Press, 1954).

3. See C. Wright Mills, *White Collar* (New York: Oxford University Press, 1951), and *The Power Elite* (New York: Oxford University Press, 1957); and Louis Wirth, "Urbanism as a Way of Life," *American Journal of Sociology* 44 (July 1938): 3–24, reprinted in Paul K. Hatt and Albert J. Riess, Jr., eds., *Cities and Society* (Glencoe, Ill.: Free Press, 1959), pp. 46–63. For a comparative national framework within which to conceptualize local communities, see chap. 3, below.

local policy-making. The relative integration of a power structure is classified according to these categories:

(1) *Elite:* A single unified group or person controls all community decisions, all of the time.

(2) *Weak elite:* A person or a single unified group controls some community decisions, some of the time.

(3) *Quasi-elite:* Leadership in all community decisions comes from a delimitable aggregate or list of persons who are not a unified group.

(4) *Weak quasi-elite:* Leadership in some, but not all, community decisions comes from persons who do not constitute a unified group, but are limited enough in number to be defined as an aggregate or list.

(5) *Ecology of games:* No person, group, or delimitable aggregate of persons controls regularly in even some decisions.

There is also an open-ended category which is used for other cases.

Power structures are commonly viewed in terms of their shapes. In addition to the elite categorization, a power structure can be classified as one of the following shapes: pyramidal, multi-pyramidal, fluid group alliances, varying according to issues, and factional. Again, an open-ended option exists for shape. Using both the elite and the shape conceptualizations, nine operational dichotomous attributes are constructed. These are numbered in the range from #83 to #93. Examples are found in Table 2–1 (var. #85) and Table 2–9 (vars. #83, #87, and #91).

For simplicity, throughout this report, power structures are referred to as concentrated or pluralistic. Some familiar synonyms for "concentrated" are elite, pyramidal, monolithic, integrated, stable, highly structured, coordinated, rational, and clustered potential. Intermediate forms are weak elite, quasi-elite, multi-pyramidal, and factional. "Pluralistic" power structures are frequently labeled weak quasi-elite, ecology of games, varies according to issues, fluid, unconcentrated, unintegrated, unstable, variegated, uncoordinated, amorphous, or diffused.

In a replication study of "Community A," David A. Booth and Charles R. Adrian hypothesize that partly because of a changing economic and ecological base, the community power complex will be more variegated in 1961 than in 1954.[4] Robert O. Schulze develops a similar idea: "The basic assumption was that as the functional relationship of the community to the larger society changes, so does the nature and form of its control structure. . . . In the community relatively self-contained and uninvolved in the larger social and economic system, the community with few and scattered commitments beyond its border, local power would tend to be structured as a pyramid and heavily concentrated at the apex."[5] *Hypothesis: A trend exists toward less concentrated power structures.*

TABLE 2-1. The Trend Is Toward Less Concentrated
Community Power Structures

	#85* Decision-making structure is	
	Other than fluid group alliances, or variable according to issues (concentrated)	Fluid group alliances, or variable according to issues (pluralistic)
#1* Cities in the year		
1945 or later	65% (66)**	93% (51)
1944 or earlier	35% (35)	7% (4) P = 0.000
#2* Cities in the year		
1955 or later	43% (43)	58% (32)
1954 or earlier	57% (58)	42% (23) P = 0.068

* Variable numbers, used for cross-reference among tables in this and other publications.
** Parenthesized number is the number of cases which have the attributes represented by the cell. Percentages are calculated for columns. N's vary among tables because data are not always available for each city or are not relevant to the table.

Results: Data are highly supportive of the hypothesis. Table 2–1 offers one of nine measures of power structure, which is cross-classified with two time dichotomies. The table shows that a greater proportion of communities have fluid power structures (less concentrated) at later rather than earlier points in time. The end of World War II appears to be an important cutting point for the trend for communities to have more fluid power structures. The earlier period shows 35 cities concentrated and 4 pluralistic, whereas later there are 66 concentrated and 51 pluralistic, a very changed ratio indeed. When we dichotomize ten years later, the

4. "Power Structure and Community Change: A Replication Study of Community A," *Midwest Journal of Political Science* 6 (August 1962): 288, 291.
5. "The Role of Economic Dominants in Community Power Structure," *American Sociological Review* 23 (February 1958): 4.

shift to pluralism continues, but not as dramatically. For the 1944–45 split, all nine measures (eight not presented here) are significantly associated with time, and for the 1954–55 split, seven of nine measures (six not presented here) are significantly associated with time. Table 2–1 is unbiased. Despite systematic bias in other correlations not presented, the trend continues to exist when measurement biases are evaluated.

Trends and Participation

There is growing agreement that political leadership should not be studied exclusively either through formal or informal processes. Both should be studied together. Robert T. Daland believes that informal relationships—the total pattern of unplanned relationships, perhaps implicit ones—have assumed substantial importance in that they affect, and in some cases determine, what is done in formal institutions of government: "If this statement is a correct premise, then many actions affecting political leadership will be occurring constantly even in the smallest communities."[6]

In regard to the relatively self-contained community which tends to have local power as a pyramid, Schulze says: "More specifically, it was surmised that those persons who exercised major control over the community's economic system would tend to be the same persons who exercised preponderant control over its socio-political system. . . . With increasing urbanization . . . the economic dominants would begin to withdraw their interest. . . . As this occurred, the local power structure would in effect bifurcate—with those who exercised primary direction over its socio-political system no longer being essentially the same set of persons who exercised primary control over its economic system" (p. 4).

Though not presented, data show an increasing proportion of cities having only economic dominants as the most important participants in the power structure. Measures of both variables share systematic biases.[7] When one control factor is held constant, the relationship continues to hold: An increase is found in the proportion of cities having informals participating in the power structure rather than cities having only politicians. Informals are defined as

6. *Dixie City: A Portrait of Political Leadership* (Tuscaloosa: University of Alabama Press, 1956), p. 36.

7. Some control factors that are seriously correlated with "Who participates in the upper levels of power?" are also seriously associated with dates of studies. See Gilbert, "Study of Community Power Studies."

persons who are not holding either elective or appointive political offices and include economic dominants. No trend is found for an increased proportion of cities having both politicians and economic dominants as the most important participants in policy-making. A trend is found, however, for an increase in proportion of cities having participation from all sectors. Table 2–2 shows that, prior to 1945, no participation from all sectors was found. After 1945, eight cities have such participation. Seven of them are metropolitan central cities.

TABLE 2–2. No Cities Were Reported to Have Participation from All Sectors Prior to 1945

	#1 Cities in the year		
	1944 or earlier	1945 or later	
#106 Upper level power leaders are			
From all sectors or pressure groups and aldermanic blocs	0% (0)	8% (8)	
Other than from all sectors or pressure groups and aldermanic blocs	100% (38)	92% (94)	P = 0.108

An interpretation of the increase of economic dominants is that it is caused by changes in communities such as suburbs, rural areas, and nondiversified towns. When taking the local polity as the unit of analysis, policy-making by informals is increasing. When considering conditions under which most people in the United States live (large cities), this would probably not be the case.

Harry M. Scoble sees a trend (suburbanization, bifurcation, fragmentation) in American and perhaps Canadian politics related to the decline of the political boss, and he offers reasons for the latter: (1) tremendous growth in leisure time and opportunity for "creative realization of the self," (2) automation, (3) geographical mobility, and (4) increasing distribution of higher education.[8] (Decline of political bosses is supported in a subsequent section.)

Trends, Institutions, and Organizations

Newspapers are classified in the current study as a community institution, as are business, school, church, and voluntary associa-

8. "Some Questions for Researchers," in Robert S. Cahill and Stephen P. Hencley, eds., *The Politics of Education in the Local Community* (Danville, Ill.: Interstate Printers and Publishers, Inc., 1964), p. 123.

tions. Hindsight would keep each class separate, but, alas, it is too late to change the current analysis. Edward C. Banfield and James Q. Wilson predict that civic leaders (especially paid executives of civic associations), associations, and the press will increase their influence: "These institutions speak (or claim to speak) from expertise with regard to 'objective facts,' and to represent a conception of the public interest."[9] *Hypothesis: Institutions and organizations have become more important in shaping community policy over time.*

Results: A trend is not found. Because the measure might be weak, the question should remain open. (One might interpret Table 2–2 as supportive.)

Trends and Functions of Local Government

We may think of local government as having one of two functions or orientations. (1) The political function mediates conflict between various interests in the community. "Political" cities tend to have partisan elections, ward voting, and political machines. These characteristics are thought to be congenial to the "self-serving" immigrant, ethnic, or working-class ideal and to machine-style, conflict-oriented politics. (2) The "good" government function stresses businesslike efficiency and absence of graft and "corruption," and often assumes that no conflicts of interest exist in the community. The term "good" should not be taken as the endorsement of such governments, but rather should be understood as a commonly used label. Good government cities tend to have nonpartisan, at-large elections and a manager form of government. These characteristics are congenial to the "public-serving" interests of the Protestant or middle-class ideal.[10]

About one-fourth of the cities analyzed here have been classified as a mixture of both orientations. A slightly smaller number are conflict oriented (the political function) and slightly more than half are good government.

Banfield and Wilson say: "Although the spread of the middle-class ideal may reduce local government's ability to manage conflict, it will also reduce the amount of conflict requiring management and make easier the management of such as there is. . . . [Conflicts] will be relatively easy to manage . . . because they

9. *City Politics* (Cambridge: Harvard University Press, 1965), p. 334.
10. Ibid., passim.

will concern the merits of concrete issues, not generalized class antagonisms. What is more, the content of the middle-class ideal is such as to make the management of conflict easier, for the ideal includes willingness to settle matters on the basis of reasonable discussion and to make sacrifices of immediate and private interest for the sake of the longer-run 'larger good of the community as a whole' " (p. 341). *Hypothesis: No difference should be found in the level and ability to manage conflict by governments of disparate functions.* That is, no difference should be found between the old style (the political function) and the new style (good government function) politics. The hypothesis, as presented, is not directly derived from the quotation immediately above, but is deduced from the premise that governments oriented toward the political function are better able to handle conflict when it arises.

Results: The hypothesis is strongly contradicted. Conflict appears to be much better handled or less prevalent in towns having an orientation toward good government, as shown in Table 2–3. Among good government cities, 14 have high or medium conflict and 54 do not. Among cities having a machine politics orientation, 34 have high or medium conflict and 22 do not.

Conflict here was measured by answer to the following question: "Degree of community conflict present, and how is it handled?" Final coding is as follows:

low conflict = no conflict, even covert (7 cases);
medium-low = any conflict present is handled well by institutional channels, or no conflict reported at all (83 cases);
medium = conflict not handled as well as in medium-low, but better than in high, or conflict is between those in top power positions (48 cases);
high = there is serious conflict with permanent splits among persons and groups within the community (5 cases).

The reader might be interested in knowing that among high-conflict cities, unemployment rates tend to be considerably higher and population size tends to be greater than among low-conflict cities. Among good government cities, those oriented primarily toward keeping taxes low tend to have less conflict than those oriented toward increasing services and toward community development and growth.

Banfield and Wilson see a general trend away from the conflict and machine-style ethos as a result of changes in the class composition of the urban electorate. Increasingly, rule is by the "qualified" rather than by the "politicians." Though population with Anglo-Saxon Protestant values is increasing on the fringes of cities

TABLE 2–3. Good Government Cities Have Less Conflict

	#99 Degree of community conflict is		
	High or medium	Medium low or low	
#75 Local government is oriented toward			
Good government	29% (14)	71% (54)	
Mixed good government and machine politics, or machine politics	71% (34)	29% (22)	P = 0.000

and central cities remain the homes of "immigrants," these values are expected to prevail through state and federal governments which take away patronage from the central cities and thereby undo machine politics (pp. 329–30). *Hypothesis: The trend is away from machine politics toward good government.*

Results: Data support the notion that governments are increasingly taking on the good government function, as shown in Table 2–4. This table shows that the percentage of cities whose local governments are oriented only to machine politics has decreased from 39 per cent prior to 1945 to 15 per cent in 1945 and later. If we take 1954–55 as a cutoff point, the decrease in percentage is from 30 per cent to 14 per cent. Data quality control analysis of Table 2–4 reveals that the data for the 1944–45 split are systematically biased, but not the data for the 1954–55 split.

Trends and Government Experts

Banfield and Wilson state, "Politicians will try to look more and more like city managers. . . . The same forces that push the politician in this direction [the middle class ideal] will draw professional administrators into politics . . ." (p. 333). *Hypothesis: Experts will increasingly recommend policy rather than legitimate it.*

Results: No support is found for the prediction, using a measure which classified the place of experts in recommending policy or legitimating it. Another measure asks, "Who enforces innovation in the community?" Table 2–5 shows that the tendency since 1945 is for innovation to be enforced by pressure groups, informals, the electorate, or various segments of the community depending upon the innovation, rather than by government officials and their

TABLE 2–4. The Trend Is Away from Machine Politics

	#1 Cities in the year		#2 Cities in the year	
	1944 or earlier	1945 or later	1954 or earlier	1955 or later
#76 Local government is oriented toward				
Machine politics	39% (14)	15% (14)	30% (19)	14% (9)
Good government or mixed good government and machine politics	61% (22)	85% (77)	70% (44)	86% (55)
	P = 0.008		P = 0.034	

TABLE 2–5. Innovation Is Decreasingly Enforced by Government Officials and Their Agencies

	#1 In the year		
	1944 or earlier	1945 or later	
#125 Innovation is enforced by			
Government officials and their agencies	66% (21)	38% (32)	
Pressure groups, the electorate, informals, or various segments depending on issues	34% (11)	62% (52)	P = 0.012

agencies. The latter are important in only 38 per cent of cities after 1945, whereas before then, they enforced innovation in 66 per cent of cities studied. Data quality control analysis reveals that both measures used in Table 2–5 share a systematic error (which is not controlled and is therefore suspect).

2. Dimensions of Power Structure

While section 1 deals with trends and subsequent sections deal with relationships between underlying community characteristics and power structures, this section deals with interrelated features of power structures, per se. One area of continuing concern to power theorists is the real nature of a community's power structure, especially whether it is relatively elitist and integrated, or pluralistic. Elsewhere, I offer a framework which indicates the variability of community decision-making processes, and a critique of an "either/or" approach to the subject.[11]

Conditions for Democracy

Hypothesis: Terry N. Clark offers the following among thirty-four interrelated hypotheses he inventories: "*The greater the number of effective competing political parties (or factions within a single party in a one-party community), the more pluralistic the power structure.*"[12] An alternative formulation is offered by Edwin H. Rhyne. In his study of "Lincoln," "Bryan," and "Jefferson" counties, he attempts to disprove or modify the theory that more political organization (the two-party system) makes for a more democratic process.[13]

Results: Using measures of power structure, it is found that Clark's hypothesis is supported. Cities which are dominated by one political party tend to have very concentrated power structures (see Table 2–6). Fifty-four per cent of cities dominated by one political party have pyramidal power structures, whereas 28 per cent of cities not dominated by one party are pyramidal. (Though containing bias, measure #90, Elite, obtains similar results.) However, because of the juxtaposition of the concepts of pluralism and democratic process, a more detailed analysis is useful. Although not presented here, my data show that cities which are dominated by one political party tend also to have party elections, ward electoral systems, strong control by politicians, machine-oriented governments, and not to have city managers. In cities dominated by the Republican Party, the power structures tend to be closed. In those dominated by the Democratic Party, power structures tend to be open, or open to a particular ethnic group in the community.

Data show further that where neither political party dominates, cities tend to have good government orientation, city managers, nonpartisan, at-large elections, and weak politicians and political parties. The power structures tend to be composed of fluid group alliances, not to be closed, but open especially to Anglos.

11. Gilbert, "Community Power Structure," chaps. 2 and 5.
12. Clark, ed., *Community Structure and Decision-Making: Comparative Analyses* (San Francisco: Chandler Publishing Co., 1968), p. 125. My italics.
13. "Political Parties and Decision-Making in Three Southern Counties," *American Political Science Review* 52 (December 1958): 1091–1107. (Rhyne's study is not included in the data of the current inquiry because he investigated counties, not cities.)

I find it difficult to interpret all of the above findings in terms of democracy or pluralism because the picture is not homogeneous. Is a concentrated power structure open to all social types less pluralistic (or more democratic) than a fluid structure closed to many sectors of the population?

TABLE 2-6. ONE-PARTY DOMINATION IS ASSOCIATED WITH
CONCENTRATED POWER

	#67 Local policy is dominated by		
	One political party	Both major political parties, or neither political party	
#83 Decision-making structure is			
Other than a single pyramid	46% (11)	72% (59)	
A single pyramid	54% (13)	28% (23)	P = 0.027

*Candidate Selection, Participation, and
Party Domination*

From their study of Florida cities, Gladys M. Kammerer and John DeGrove[14] were able to make the following generalization: "Economic, social and political groups that help them [elected or appointed officials] achieve their officeholding status enjoy an 'access' to such officeholders which makes them participants in the exercise of power also."[15] *Hypothesis: Groups that select candidates also participate in the power structure.*

Results: Table 2–7 can be interpreted as highly supportive of the hypothesis. All relationships are as predicted. Two cross-classifications (#104 × #109 and #112) share measurement error on both variables. Since the large majority of correlations are "safe," the following statements hold as a summarization of the table. (1) When politicians at least partly select candidates, or political committees exclusively select candidates, power structures tend

14. "Urban Leadership During Change," *The Annals* 353 (May 1964): 95–106. This study resulted also in the following publications: Gladys M. Kammerer and John M. DeGrove, *Florida City Managers* (Gainesville: University of Florida, 1961); Gladys M. Kammerer, Charles D. Farris, John M. DeGrove, and Alfred B. Clubok, *City Managers in Politics* (Gainesville: University of Florida Monographs, Social Sciences, no. 13, 1962); and the same four authors, *The Urban Political Community: Profiles in Town Politics* (Boston: Houghton Mifflin, 1963).
15. "Urban Leadership," p. 99.

TABLE 2–7. GROUPS THAT SELECT CANDIDATES TEND TO DOMINATE POLICY

Formal political structure is really	#67 Local policy is dominated by		#102 Structure is headed by		#104 Upper-level power leaders are	
	One political party	Both major political parties, or neither major political party	Officials only	Officials and nonofficials, or nonofficials only	Politicians only	Not politicians only
#109 Selected by politicians, at least in part	100% (20)	45% (25)	71% (27)	52% (28)	70% (26)	52% (24)
Not selected by politicians, at least in part	0% (0)	55% (31) P = 0.000	29% (11)	48% (26) P = 0.085	30% (11)	48% (22) P = 0.117
#110 Selected by a political committee only	90% (18)	18% (10)	63% (24)	18% (10)	60% (22)	20% (9)
Not selected by a political committee only	10% (2)	82% (46) P = 0.000	37% (14)	82% (44) P = 0.000	40% (15)	80% (37) P = 0.000
#111 Selected by civic and informal leaders	0% (0)	20% (11)	8% (3)	20% (11)	5% (2)	24% (11)
Not selected by civic and informal leaders	100% (20)	80% (45) P = 0.032	92% (35)	80% (43) P = 0.142	95% (35)	76% (35) P = 0.032
#112 Selected by both political and informal leaders, not necessarily cooperatively	P > alpha — Democrats never dominate when both politicals and informals select		8% (3)	33% (18)	11% (4)	33% (15)
Not selected by both political and informal leaders			92% (35)	67% (36) P = 0.005	89% (33)	67% (31) P = 0.021
#113 Selected by no one—candidate builds own organization, typically	0% (0)	21% (12)	P > alpha		P > alpha	
Selected—candidate does not build his own organization	100% (20)	79% (44) P = 0.029			Informals only are never upper-level leaders when candidates build own organization	

to be headed by officials, upper-level leaders tend to be politicians only, and one-party domination is the rule. (2) When civic and informal leaders partly or exclusively choose candidates, officials are rarely exclusive heads of power structures, politicians tend to share upper-level leadership with others if they are involved in it at all, and one-party domination is rare. (3) When the typical mode is for a candidate to build his own organization, one-party domination is never found and informals are never upper-level leaders. (4) When both political and informal leaders select candidates, the Democratic Party never dominates.

Politics and Newspapers

Political scientists often consider newspapers an important element in a community political system. For example, Scoble includes them in a list of important variables and says, "The number and competitiveness of mass media, particularly the printed newspapers in the community, could be of extreme significance for local politics" (p. 117). The significance of newspapers is spelled out by Reo M. Christenson: "Even a shrewd and generally respected monopoly newspaper appears unable to shape local opinion when voters are strongly predisposed to favor a given course of action or inaction. But where they are closely divided, or, more commonly, apathetic, *The Blade*'s experience suggests that a newspaper which knows what it's about can often carry the day."[16] Experience, such as that of early 1960 Miami, further adds to the impression that newspapers are important for recommending candidates and policies when the public is poorly organized politically.

Because no separate measure of the importance of newspapers was included in the current study, the measure of control of local policies by institutional and organizational sectors (which includes newspapers) is explored. Using degree of community conflict as a measure of voter division, no significant association is found. Another measure, the importance of the masses, is associated with the importance of institutions and organizations. Table 2–8 shows a tendency for masses to be relatively weak in cities where organizations and institutions have little control over policy. Fifty-three per cent of cities in which institutions and organizations have control over local policies are also those whose populations defeat the ad-

16. "The Power of the Press: The Case of 'The Toledo Blade,'" *Midwest Journal of Political Science* 3 (August 1959): 239.

ministration or power structure on at least one referendum, or are those whose populations are important for some issues. The opposite side of the picture is that 71 per cent of the organizationally weak cities have populations that are acquiescent, supportive, or weak in relation to leaders, or populations that are involved in only neighborhood interests. There is a discrepancy between the measures used here and Christenson's ideas, so that the latter are not really tested, but provide a basis for exploring data.

TABLE 2-8. APATHY IS MORE COMMON WHERE COMMUNITY
INSTITUTIONS ARE WEAK

	#82 Control of local policies by institutional and organizational sectors is		
	Strong or moderate	Weak	
#123 Populations			
Are acquiescent, supportive, or weak in relation to leaders, or involved in neighborhood interests	47% (40)	71% (10)	
Have defeated the administration or power structure on at least one referendum, or are important for some issues	53% (45)	29% (4)	P = 0.148

Power Structure and the Function of Local Government

David Rogers compiled a list of conditions under which political systems will be monolithic or pluralistic. When the scope of government is extensive, the system will be pluralistic, and, of course, when the scope is limited, monolithic.[17] *Hypothesis: A local government which has more than one function is wider in scope than a government having one function and it will therefore tend to be more pluralistic.*

Results: Questionable support is found for the hypothesis. When good government cities are compared to all other cities, no differences in structure are found. In comparing cities having the political function to other cities, the former tend to have concentrated structures, as shown in Table 2–9. The table uses three measures of concentration. It shows that 54 per cent of cities with govern-

17. "Community Political Systems," in Bert Swanson, ed., *Current Trends in Comparative Community Studies* (Kansas City, Mo.: Community Studies, Inc., 1962), p. 47.

ments oriented toward machine politics have single pyramids and 26 per cent of other cities have them. Sixty-nine per cent of politically oriented governments have a group structure as compared to 41 per cent of other cities. Finally, 69 per cent of the politically oriented governments have an elite or weak elite as compared to 40 per cent of cities with good governments or governments of mixed function. Support must be accepted cautiously, partly be-

TABLE 2-9. CONCENTRATED STRUCTURES OCCUR PROPORTIONATELY MORE OFTEN AMONG GOVERNMENTS ORIENTED TOWARD MACHINE POLITICS

	#76 Whose local government is oriented toward		
	Good government, or mixed good government and machine politics	Machine politics	
#83 Decision-making structure is			
A single pyramid	26% (26)	54% (14)	
Other than a single pyramid	74% (72)	46% (12)	P = 0.017
#87 Top decision-makers are			
A group	41% (40)	69% (18)	
Not a group	59% (58)	31% (8)	P = 0.014
#91 Top decision-makers are			
An elite or weak elite	40% (35)	69% (18)	
A quasi-elite, weak quasi-elite, or an ecology of games	60% (53)	31% (8)	P = 0.013

cause all measures share one systematic error in measurement. In addition, among cities with the political function, power structures are probably distributed curvilinearly, i.e., politically oriented systems tend to be found among both the most monolithic and most pluralistic, whereas the middle of the continuum is occupied with cities oriented toward good government and political functions. None of the above, however, invalidates Rogers' hypothesis, because scope of government is actually a more inclusive concept than is the measure used here.

Power Structure and Participation

An interesting problem is the relationship between power structures and the characteristics of people or sectors of the community which head them. Thus we find disparate views not only about whether structures are really elitist or pluralistic, but also— given one or the other—about whether it is the political officials who really lead or other persons who influence policy even while not holding formal office.

Delbert C. Miller proposes, "Businessmen exert a predominant influence in community decision making."[18] Nelson W. Polsby attempts to refute: "The upper class rules in community life." In objecting to the hypothesis that a single power elite rules in the community, Polsby reasons as follows: where a general elite would be found, it would place great emphasis on the maintenance of sociability and contact with a wide range of citizens in the community and less emphasis on accomplishment. The members of an elite would restrict their own activities. Any elite group wanting to innovate or put programs into effect would fail unless it acquired consent (i.e., legitimacy) from nonelite members of the community. Further, in areas of concern to them, nonelites seek to bring elites under control.[19]

From discussions, one might get the impression that if there is a single ruling group in a community, it must be composed of business or social leaders. Clark offers a hypothesis, though, which shifts the emphasis in such a way that low involvement of business elites might result in less pluralism: "The lower the involvement of business elites in community activities beyond a certain minimal point, the smaller the number of competing elites and the less pluralistic the power structure" (p. 125). Although terminology changes, another popular image is that centralized leaders are public officials rather than socialites or economic dominants. In his study of Edgewood and Riverview, Robert Presthus reports whether hypotheses he gathered up and listed are supported. These include two derived from the work of Dahl: (1) A leader in one issue area is not likely to be influential in another. (This is not supported by Presthus' findings.) (2) If he is, he is probably a public official and most likely the mayor. (This is partially supported by Presthus' findings.[20])

18. "Industry and Community Power Structure: A Comparative Study of an American and an English City," *American Sociological Review* 23 (February 1958): 11.

19. *Community Power and Political Theory* (New Haven: Yale University Press, 1963), p. 10.

20. *Men at the Top* (New York: Oxford University Press, 1964), p. 420.

The basis for the image of the politician's central importance was discussed at a conference of metropolitan political leadership. Papers were prepared by Rossi, Dahl, Kaufman, and Long:

> There was general agreement among the participants that the contemporary American setting fosters a fragmented distribution of power resources and that, with some exceptions, if any integrated leadership exists it is likely to be found in the formally elected officials.
>
> Any tendency toward a high degree of influence over most or all sectors of community policy, Dahl suggested, is likely to be associated with the group of elected public officials who have ample resources and the skill and incentives to use them copiously and efficiently. The tendency toward a concentration of influence, wherever it may occur, reflects the disposition of all groups to use their resources relatively sparingly in the sphere of public policy, and thus for those few who employ them more frequently and fully to be especially influential. Coalitions of elite "chieftains," in Dahl's view, may appear when these leaders feel the need for a degree of coordination not supplied by their "independent sovereignties"; but such coalitions are not likely to develop without a "political entrepreneur" as coalition builder. For this role the chief elected executive is the expected candidate. Under appropriate conditions such a coalition may develop into a persisting executive-centered order, a coalition of coalitions, in which the elected chief executive is the only individual of high influence in all the groups.[21]

Elsewhere I hypothesized: "The more concentrated the power structure, the greater is the likelihood that informals carry out community political functions; obversely . . . pluralistic . . . politicians."[22]

After rigorous testing and subsequent analysis, the hypothesis was revised as follows: *The more concentrated the power structure, the greater is the tendency for the top decision-makers to come from one segment of the community: politics, business, society and/or labor. Obversely, the more pluralistic the power*

21. David B. Truman, "Theory and Research on Metropolitan Political Leadership: Report on a Conference," *Items* 15 (New York: Social Science Research Council, March 1961): 2, 3.
22. "Community Power Structure," p. 30.

structure, the greater is the tendency for top decision-makers to come from many segments of the community.[23]

I found that the degree of concentration of the decision-making structure simply does not determine participation in the power structure of either business, politics, civic leadership, or other sectors. Rather, the degree of concentration correlates with whether the leaders will be from one or more sectors of the community. More than one-third of the cities have two or more sectors represented in the upper levels of policy-making or as heads of power structures. Twenty-four per cent of cities analyzed have only economic dominants as the most important participants in the power structure, but these cities tend to be under 100,000, so it seems to follow that less than 24 per cent of people in the United States live in such cities. If one sector of the community dominates policy-making, as shown later, it tends to be composed of elected and appointed officials in large or economically diversified cities and nonofficials in small or nondiversified cities.

Despite the popular belief in the strength of labor, academicians pay relatively far more attention to the place of business and politics in community rule. Perhaps this is because very few cities in the United States really have organized labor so politically strong that it dominates community decisions. Clark includes labor in his propositional inventory as follows: The better organized and more active the labor movement in the community, the more pluralistic the power structure—up to the point where the labor organizations exert such extensive influence that other groups withdraw from community activities (p. 125).

Eight of the cities analyzed have participation for the power structure from all sectors: All can be described as fluid group alliances (pluralistic). Assuming that labor participates with other sectors in these eight cities, support is given to Clark's hypothesis that organized and active labor (or other groups) contribute to a pluralistic power structure.

Four cities analyzed have either union personnel or low-income sectors as the most important participants in local decision-making. (Union personnel and low-income sectors were lumped together into one category for coding purposes.) These cities may be characterized neither as having an elite so strong that it dominates all policy, nor as being so pluralistic that no groups or individuals are

23. Ibid., p. 57, and below.

consistently involved in policy-making. The only identical charac-
teristic shared by the four cities is that they are all located in the
North Central region as defined by the U.S. Census. St. Paul and
Minneapolis are two of them. The other two are located in the
East North Central subregion and share all of the following characteristics: economies are dominated by one to three industries,
median income is above the U.S. average, population growth rate
is 0–4 per cent in the decade during which they were investigated,
mayor-council is the form of government, orientation of local government is to both the political and good government function,
power structure is almost completely open to all social types, and
conflict is well handled by institutional channels.

3. ECONOMIC FUNCTION OF A COMMUNITY

Students of politics and social structure have often observed a
relationship between the way people in a community earn a living
and the form that is taken by politics. In this section we consider
the way people earn a living as the economic function of the community, and present hypotheses relevant to the economic function.

Economic Function and Power Structure

Theorists predict power structure on the basis of the economic
function of a city: an increase in either "industrialization" or "economic diversity" results in an increase of pluralism.[24] Diversity is
usually posited in contrast to economies of the following types:
specialized, farm, dependence on nearby cities for employment,
and domination by one or a few industries. Delbert C. Miller states
that the less diversified the economic base of a community, the
more clustered is the potential for power,[25] and dominance by one
function (church, government, or education) in a town has consequences for the institutional power arrangements.[26] *Hypothesis:*

24. Clark, pp. 124–25; Delbert C. Miller and William H. Form, *Industry,
Labor and Community* (New York: Harper and Brothers, 1960); John Walton, "Substance and Artifact: The Current Status of Research on Community Power Structure," *American Journal of Sociology* 71 (January 1966):
435; Presthus, p. 46; and Lawrence D. Mann, "Studies in Community Decision-
Making," *American Institute of Planners Journal* 30 (February 1964): 62.
25. "Democracy and Decision Making in the Community Power Structure,"
in William D'Antonio and Howard J. Ehrlich, eds., *Power and Democracy
in America* (Notre Dame, Ind.: University of Notre Dame Press, 1961), p. 62.
26. "Town and Gown: The Power Structure of a University Town,"
American Journal of Sociology 68 (January 1963): 432.

The more diversified the economic function of the city, the greater is the tendency toward a pluralistic power structure; obversely . . . nondiversified . . . concentrated.

Results: The hypothesis as stated is not supported. It is surprising to find no support for the relationship between economic diversity and power structure, for such a hypothesis has been advanced so frequently. Detailed analysis appearing elsewhere[27] compares economically diversified cities with other cities, using three objective scales and one judgmental measure of economic function of a city. Of 36 operationalizations of the hypothesis, 32 did not reach alpha, 1 was supportive, and 3 were disconfirming to it. None were strong associations, and they might have been due to chance. Hence, I concluded that economic function of a city is not a predictor of integration of a political system nor is it consistently related to the shape of power structure.

Both because of the theoretical importance of economic function and because the prediction as stated above might be too crude to achieve results, a correlation matrix is combed to see if any light can be shed: of 72 correlations (9 measures of power structure, 8 measures of economic function), 9 are beyond $P = 0.150$. This number can be expected by chance, but it is instructive to examine some of the tables. Summarizing an analysis that appears elsewhere, it can be said that (1) functional metropolises tend to be ecologically (pluralistically) structured, and (2) cities specialized in manufacturing or finance tend to have group, elite, and weak elite structures.[28] No association is found among any measures of power structure when cross-classified with the following four measures of economic function: diversified (Nelson classification) (see note 28); judged diversified; farm, farm trade, or mixed farming; and dominated by one, two, or three industries.

Cities whose economies are dependent on nearby areas for em-

27. Gilbert, "Community Power Structure," p. 55 and chap. 4, passim.
28. Ibid. Functional metropolis refers to "super, mature, or limited metropolises" rather than "partial metropolis, local service center, average city, regional or local subcenter, or satellite cities." See Robert L. Carroll, "The Metropolitan Influence of the 168 Standard Area Central Cities," *Social Forces* 42 (December 1963): 166–73. Specialized in manufacturing or finance is in contrast to diversified or specialized in other than manufacturing or finance. See Howard A. Nelson, "A Service Classification of American Cities," *Economic Geography* 31 (July 1955): 189–210. Manufacturing and finance cities, as classified by Nelson's technique, tend to be the cities that are judgmentally referred to as "diversified" in the current study.

ployment tend to have concentrated power structures (see Table 2–10). Five of six of these cities have a group structure of power, half of them have an elite structure, and three of four have low conflict. Among all other cities, only 39 per cent have a group structure of power, 16 per cent have an elite, and 4 per cent have low conflict.

TABLE 2-10. WHEN PEOPLE DEPEND ON NEARBY TOWNS FOR WORK, THEIR OWN TOWNS TEND TO HAVE A GROUP STRUCTURE AND LITTLE CONFLICT

	#41 Economic base is judged		
	Dependent on nearby area for work	Other than dependent on nearby area for work	
#87 Top decision-makers are			
A group	83% (5)	39% (48)	
Not a group	17% (1)	61% (76)	P = 0.081
#90 Top decision-makers are			
An elite	50% (2)	16% (17)	
A weak elite, quasi-elite, weak quasi-elite, or an ecology of games	50% (2)	84% (89)	P = 0.137
#100 Degree of community conflict is			
High, medium, or medium low	25% (1)	96% (108)	
Low	75% (3)	4% (4)	P = 0.001

There are 15 economically specialized cities included in the analysis: three college, three resort, two government and education, two retirement and resort, one military, and one retirement city. (Three are unclassified as to specialty.) In Table 2–11 it appears that specialized cities have a disproportionate share of permanent factional structures, 40 per cent as contrasted to 4 per cent of other cities. They tend not to have group or elite structures. Using two measures of concentration, we find that only 20 per cent of specialized cities have a group structure of power and 20 per cent have an elite or weak elite. Forty-four per cent of other cities have group structures and 43 per cent of them have an elite or weak elite.

Economic Function and Conflict

Data show that cities characterized by a high or medium degree of conflict tend to be diversified cities (Nelson classification of func-

tionally specialized in finance or manufacturing). No city whose
economic base is diversified (judgmental classification) is among
cities of low conflict. (Data are not presented.) On the basis of
Clark's hypothesis—"the greater the density of cross-cutting
status-sets, the more controlled the community conflicts" (p. 24)—
it is a speculation that economically diversified cities have a lower
relative density of cross-cutting status sets than other cities. Cities
whose residents are dependent upon nearby areas for work are, on
the other hand, disproportionately among those with low conflict (see Table 2–10).

TABLE 2–11. Cities with Specialized Economic Bases Tend to Have
Factional and Pluralistic Structures

	#40 Economic base is judged		
	Specialized	Other than specialized	
#86 Decision-making structure is			
Not permanent factions	60% (9)	96% (109)	
Permanent factions	40% (6)	4% (4)	P = 0.00
#87 Top decision-makers are			
A group	20% (3)	44% (50)	
Not a group	80% (12)	56% (65)	P = 0.09
#91 Top decision-makers are			
An elite, or weak elite	20% (3)	43% (41)	
A quasi-elite, weak quasi-elite, or an ecology of games	80% (12)	57% (54)	P = 0.10

Economic Growth and Power Structure

Ernest A. T. Barth develops the following generalization: "The
rapid expansion of the economic base of a community (especially
where the community population is small prior to this expansion)
is related to the development of clique structures in the influence
system."[29] The measure, "growth of the employment base," is
weak because data are missing for the overwhelming majority of
cities. No measure of power structure correlates with growth of
the economic base, but factional structures appear in cities whose
employment base has not kept up with population growth (see
Table 2–12).

29. "Community Influence Systems: Structure and Change," *Social Forces*
40 (October 1961): 58–63 (emphasis supplied).

None of the cities whose employment has kept up with population growth are characterized by factional power structures, and 22 per cent of those whose employment has not kept up with population growth are characterized by permanent factions. The numbers involved are too small to place much confidence in.

TABLE 2–12. FACTIONS MIGHT APPEAR WHERE EMPLOYMENT DOES NOT KEEP UP

	#44 Employment base has grown	
	Fast, or equal relative to population growth	Slow relative to population growth
#86 Decision-making structure is		
Permanent factions	0% (0)	22% (2)
Not permanent factions	100% (14)	78% (7) P = 0.142

TABLE 2–13. POLITICIANS ARE LESS IMPORTANT IN CITIES DOMINATED BY FEW INDUSTRIES

	#39 Economic base judged	
	Dominated by one, two, or three industries	Other than dominated by one, two, or three industries
#104 Upper-level power leaders are		
Politicians only	20% (8)	39% (28)
Not politicians only	80% (32)	61% (43) P = 0.038

Economic Function and Participation

Elsewhere I propose the hypothesis "*The greater the economic diversity of the city, the greater the likelihood the participants in the power structure are politicians; obversely . . . less diversified . . . informals.*"[30]

Results: The hypothesis is supported. Economic function predicts participation.[31] Economically diversified cities tend to have politicians as the most important participants in the structure and officials as heads.

Further analysis shows that economically specialized cities never have informals as the only important participants and never have only nonofficials as heads of structures. Cities dominated by one or few industries tend less than other cities to have only politicians

30. "Community Power Structure," p. 30.
31. Ibid., pp. 55–56.

as the most important figures in community decision-making (see Table 2–13). Twenty per cent of one-industry towns are led by politicians only, as compared to 39 per cent of other cities.

Economic Base and Class, and Political Parties

Kammerer and DeGrove analyzed conditions that favor political boss controls:

> We do not conceive of a boss as ruling in solitary splendor but simply as having a primacy in the clique due to his central position in the communications net.
>
> Much more significant from the standpoint of identifying what may well be the most important independent variables in the boss-controlled town, we found that, despite some increase in population, the town obtained no new economic bases and no new or different social classes, nor did any outside-based groups attempt to inject themselves into decision-making in the town. In contrast, neighboring communities grew very rapidly, changing in their economic and social configurations, especially in the direction of getting a large proportion of higher income and more highly educated migrants and thereby changing in their political configurations.
>
> In short, the concept of boss is tied up with exercise of actual power and is not limited to mere persuasion or to reputational attributes. It is also tied up with a particular kind of town, as to economic and social flavor—predominately working class.[32]

No measure of political bossism is included in the current work, but two of three related measures support the ideas offered in the quotation directly above. Table 2–14 has those measures of the dependent variables which support their hypotheses.

Cities whose employment bases have grown slowly are used to represent Kammerer and DeGrove's concept of "no new economic base." Such cities tend to have strong political parties, politicians dominant in decision-making, and factional structures. Some of these cities are very small, none of them is economically diversified, and the majority of them are located in the Northeast and South. As a measure of working class populations, we use the

32. "Urban Leadership," p. 98.

measure "a low proportion of the population earning over $10,-000." These cities also tend to have strong political parties, or politicians balanced in strength or in coalition with other groups. Officials tend to head up structures, and structures tend to be concentrated. These "working class" cities tend to be small metropolitan centers or small cities, lower than other cities on three measures of education, and primarily located in the South or Northeast. All of these relationships are summarized in Table 2–14.

TABLE 2–14. CITIES WITH NO NEW ECONOMIC BASES, OR WITH WORKING-CLASS CHARACTERISTICS, TEND TO BE DOMINATED BY POLITICIANS—SUMMARY

	#44 Employment base has grown slow relative to population growth	#33 Proportion of population earning over $10,000 in 1960 is low*
How strong are parties?	Strong	Balanced or coalition, or strong
Who are important?	Usually politicians only, never economic dominants only	See Table 2–16, officials or officials and nonofficials
Structure?	See Table 2–12, sometimes factional	Disproportionately elite, weak elite, or quasi-elite
What differentiates these from other cities?	Some are very small, always other than diversified, majority located in Northeast, South	Small metropolitan centers, small cities, lower than others on 3 measures of education, located in South or Northeast, primarily

* Only cities studied in 1955 or later are included here.

Disconfirming to the political bossism hypothesis are data which show that cities which have no new social classes (growth is not overrepresented by persons of lower SES and nonwhite increase is negative or low) tend to have high SES populations. The political correlates of high SES cities are inconsistent with the hypothesis of Kammerer and DeGrove, which specifies the working-class flavor of cities with bosses. It might be concluded that the working-class flavor and the lack of new employment both favor boss "rule," whereas social class change (at least as it is measured here) is irrelevant.

4. SOCIAL CHARACTERISTICS OF A COMMUNITY

Theorists hypothesize about social characteristics in either aggregate terms or in social organizational terms.

Social Characteristics and Power Structure

Walton's inventory includes a hypothesis which combines aggregate and organizational social concepts: "Socially integrated, heterogeneous populations have less concentrated power structures" (p. 435). Miller says, "The political homogeneity of a community seems to be a contributing factor in delineating power-structure and processes."[33] Rogers proposes that when the degree of heterogeneity of a population along ethnic, religious, and occupational lines is high, the power structure will be pluralistic, when low,

TABLE 2–15. Social Characteristics of Community Correlate with Power Structure Shape

	#84 Decision-making structure is		
	A single pyramid or multipyramids	Other than a single pyramid or multipyramids	
#45 Median age for census year is			
Old	37% (13)	64% (35)	
Young	63% (22)	36% (20)	P = 0.018
#46 Proportion of population under five years old for census year is			
Low	45% (30)	60% (36)	
High	55% (37)	40% (24)	P = 0.110
#52 Per cent nonwhite for any census year is			
7.51% or higher	35% (24)	56% (35)	
7.50% or lower	65% (44)	44% (28)	P = 0.023
#54 Nonwhite increase is			
Medium or high	37% (7)	63% (24)	
Negative or low	63% (12)	37% (14)	P = 0.091

monolithic. When unionization of blue-collar workers or political and economic organization of working-class groups is extensive, the system will be pluralistic, when limited, monolithic (p. 47). Clark offers the following: "The higher the educational level of community residents, the more pluralistic the power structure" (p. 126).

Walton found support, though not strong, for less concentrated structure associated with "socially integrated, heterogeneous popu-

33. "Democracy and Decision-Making," p. 52.

lations." He found no difference when using population composition (heterogeneous-homogeneous) (p. 435n18). *Hypothesis: Homogeneous populations are positively associated with concentrated power structures.*

Results: The current study uses only aggregate measures of population composition. One measure of power structure, "a single pyramid or multi-pyramids," is cross-classified with thirteen measures of population composition. Four associations are found, none of them overly strong. Cities with pyramidal power structures tend to have populations whose median age is below the average for the United States. Sixty-three per cent of them are so characterized, as compared to 36 per cent of cities that do not have pyramidal structures. The youthful populations are taken to stand for "suburban homogeneity," and it can be said that these cities tend to have concentrated structures. A high proportion of the population that is under five years old is found in 55 per cent of pyramidal cities but in only 40 per cent of the other cities. A low proportion of nonwhite population is found in 65 per cent of the pyramidally structured cities and 44 per cent of other cities. Nonwhite increase is negative or low in 63 per cent of the pyramidal cities and in 37 per cent of other cities. Other power structure measures, not presented, obtain similar results. Educational level is not associated with any measures of power structure. If population youth and nonwhite percentage and increase can be taken for measures of heterogeneity and homogeneity, it appears that the hypothesis is supported.

Social Characteristics and Participation in Leadership

Presthus suggests that in communities with limited leadership and economic resources, the power structure will more likely be dominated by political leaders, whereas in those with more fulsome internal resources, it will probably be dominated by economic leaders (pp. 410–11). *Hypothesis: In populations of higher education or wealth top leadership is more likely from nonofficial positions and, obversely, poorer and less educated populations will more likely be led by politicians and elected officials.*

Results: Characteristics of populations dominated by either politicians or economic dominants (or informals) are examined. Above average education and wealth of population appear positively associated with domination by nonofficials only. Table 2–16 shows evidence supporting the hypothesis. Eighty-three per cent of cities whose power structures are headed by nonofficials have a high proportion of their populations earning upward of $10,000 a year as compared to 52 per cent of cities handled by officials. Seventy-

TABLE 2–16. Nonofficials Are More Likely to be Politically Dominant among Wealthier and More Educated Populations

	#101 Structure is headed by		
	Officials only, or officials and nonofficials	Nonofficials only	
#33 Proportion of population earning over $10,000 in 1960 is*			
High	52% (17)	83% (10)	
Low	48% (25)	17% (2)	P = 0.058
#60 Per cent of population completing high school is			
High	37% (19)	75% (9)	
Low	63% (32)	25% (3)	P = 0.025

* Only cities studied in 1955 or later are included here.

five per cent of cities with nonofficials as heads have a high proportion of the population completing high school, as compared with only 37 per cent of other cities. No contradictions are found using other measures of participation.

Social Characteristics and Conflict

Among Presthus' many hypotheses concerning communities is "The greater the integration and value consensus, the better the constraint of conflict and the more pluralism. The more diversified the population, the more likely centralized control and conflict" (p. 412). *Hypotheses: Social characteristics correlate with degree of community conflict and centralized control and conflict are positively associated.*

Results: There is no measure of value consensus. Aggregate measures are used in Table 2–17. We find that in cities with low conflict (or conflict well handled by institutional channels), the populations tend to be wealthier, and to be more educated than those of cities with a higher degree of conflict.

Sixty-six per cent of cities with medium-low or low conflict are those whose proportion of population earning over $10,000 is high. Fifty-six per cent of cities with high or medium conflict are those with low proportions of population earning over $10,000. Seventy-four per cent of low conflict cities have populations who are educated above the median for the United States, compared with 53 per cent for higher conflict cities.

TABLE 2–17. Conflict Is Less Likely in Communities Whose Population Is More Wealthy or Educated, or Whose Decision-Making Structure Is Concentrated

| | #99 Degree of community conflict is | | |
	High or medium	Medium-low or low	
#33 Proportion of population earning over $10,000 in 1960 is			
High	44% (10)	66% (25)	
Low	56% (13)	34% (13)	P = 0.113
#58 Population is educated			
Above the U.S. median	53% (18)	74% (39)	
Below the U.S. median	47% (16)	26% (14)	P = 0.065
#83 Decision-making structure is			
A single pyramid	25% (13)	38% (33)	
Other than a single pyramid	75% (39)	62% (54)	P = 0.138

Inferring a relationship between centralized control and conflict (from Presthus), we find that of many possible associations between measures of these concepts, only one reaches alpha and it is contrary to the expectation: concentrated control systems have less conflict than do pluralistic systems. Twenty-five per cent of the higher and 38 per cent of the lower conflict cities have a single pyramidal structure (see bottom of Table 2–17).

Unfortunately the measure of conflict contains a great deal of random error, i.e., it is a weak (though probably unbiased) measure of community conflict.

Social Characteristics and the Importance of the Local Population

On the basis of his findings, Presthus believes that political participation increases with the smallness of the proportion of lower-

lower-class members in the community (p. 413). Of six measures of social class (using education and income as indicators), two correlate positively with the importance of the local population, as expected. (None measures "lower-lower-class" members of a community.) Among cities whose populations have defeated the power

TABLE 2–18. IMPORTANCE OF LOCAL POPULATION INCREASES WITH SOCIAL CLASS

#123	Populations	
	Are acquiescent, supportive, or weak in relation to leaders, or involved only in neighborhood interests	Have defeated the administration or power structure on at least one referendum, or are important for some issues
#33 Proportion of population earning over $10,000 in 1960 is		
High	44% (11)	68% (23)
Low	56% (14)	32% (11) P = 0.109
#59 Proportion of population having less than five years' education is		
Low	41% (13)	64% (28)
High	59% (19)	36% (16) P = 0.063

structure or whose populations are important, 68 per cent have a high proportion earning over $10,000 and 64 per cent have a low proportion having less than five years of education. Comparable figures for cities with politically aquiescent populations are 44 per cent with a high proportion earning over $10,000, and 41 per cent with a low proportion having less than five years of education.

Social Characteristics and Function of Local Government

Banfield and Wilson say, "In a community which is relatively compact and homogeneous . . . there is little need for 'interest balancing' . . ." (p. 25). *Hypothesis: Social characteristics which may be interpreted as indicating homogeneity and/or the middle-class ideal should be positively correlated with the good government function.*

Results: All relationships located are in the predicted direction (see Table 2–19). All three measures of education are highly and positively associated with good government. A low proportion of people earning over $10,000, a rapid growth of lower socioeconomic classes in a city, and a high proportion of foreign-born in a city all correlate positively with a government having the political function or mixed function.

5. POPULATION SIZE AND GROWTH

Population size takes a central place in theorizing about community power structures and is often used as a selection criterion by researchers interested in comparative studies. A very detailed analysis appearing elsewhere can be referred to by the reader seeking sup-

TABLE 2–19. GOOD GOVERNMENT IS MORE FREQUENTLY FOUND IN TOWNS WITH HOMOGENEOUS OR MIDDLE-CLASS POPULATION CHARACTERISTICS

	#75 Local government is oriented toward		
	Good government	Mixed good government and machine politics, or machine politics	
#33 Proportion of population earning over $10,000 in 1960 is			
Low	30% (9)	55% (16)	
High	70% (21)	45% (13)	P = 0.067
#53 Population growth is			
Overrepresented by persons of lower SES	31% (4)	82% (9)	
Not overrepresented by persons of lower SES	69% (9)	18% (2)	P = 0.019
#55 Foreign-born for any census year are			
7.6% or more	36% (21)	52% (28)	
7.5% or less	64% (37)	48% (26)	P = 0.127
#58 Population is educated			
Below U.S. median	16% (7)	60% (22)	
Above U.S. median	84% (37)	40% (15)	P = 0.000
#59 Proportion of population having less than five years' education is			
High	25% (10)	63% (22)	
Low	75% (30)	37% (13)	P = 0.001
#60 Per cent of population completing high school is			
Low	41% (12)	76% (22)	
High	59% (17)	24% (7)	P = 0.016

port for some of the generalizations found in this section.[34] Over-all results indicate that population size is important because it is highly associated with other variables that predict power structure and participation. As an interesting aside, features of research (data quality control variables) are frequently and highly associated with population size. On the other hand, population growth rate, though less frequently theorized about, should become a relevant variable in its own right as it is correlated with political features of communities more often and more strongly than is size. Because this paper is devoted to the inventorying and testing of already existing hypotheses, growth rates are not fully explored here.

Population Size and Power Structure

Both Schulze and Miller believe the size of community population is related to differences in power structures. Janowitz specifies the association as follows: "As the size of the city increases, the amount of overlap of leadership in various areas declines." Mann views size together with economic function as a determinant of structure. Rogers predicts the association of large population size with pluralis-tic systems, and small population with monolithic systems. How-ever, neither Agger nor Walton find correlation between population size and structure.[35] *Hypothesis: The larger the population size, the more likely the power structure is pluralistic; obversely . . . . . . smaller . . . concentrated.*

Results: "No contradictions occur in cross-clarifications of popu-lation size and power structure measures. Twelve percent of the co-efficients reach alpha as predicted, moderately supporting the . . . hypothesis.

"Measures of power structure do not reach alpha with measure number 26 'more than 5,000 population.' Measures of concentrated power structure do not reach alpha with any population dichot-omy. Other power structure measures (numbers 84, 85, and 89) are associated with population size: 100,000 is the strongest cutting point; fluid group alliances is the most discriminating measure of power structures in tests of [the] hypothesis.

34. Gilbert, "Community Power Structure," passim, especially pp. 26, 29, 53–54, 59–60, 63–73. See also Gilbert, "Communities, Power Structures, and Research Bias."
35. Compare Gilbert, "Community Power Structure," p. 26; Presthus, pp. 45–46; and Kammerer and DeGrove, *Florida City Managers*, p. 30.

"An interpretation is that fluid structures appear more frequently in large cities, but the location of concentrated power structures is not predicted by population size."[36]

Nine of ten cities having greater than 100,000 population and a pyramidal power structure also have only politicians as the most important participants; the other city has a combination of politicians and others. All of seven cities having more than 100,000 population and an elite structure also have officials only as head of the structure. The notions of Dahl are strongly supported: if there is a clique in a big city, it will most likely be headed by the mayor or other political officials.

No matter what city size, fluid structures are not likely to be headed exclusively by either officials or nonofficials. Factions are never headed only by nonofficials. Although there are few to generalize from, factions in large cities tend to be headed by officials only, and in smaller cities factional structures tend to be led by a combination of officials and others. In the large city, multipyramidal structures do not tend to have only nonofficials as heads. In any cities, pyramidal structures tend most to be headed by elected officials, but the tendency is greatest in cities of large population.

Pyramids are headed by nonofficials about one-fourth of the time, but in cities of more than 100,000, any combination of officials and nonofficials is rare, whereas combinations occur about 25 per cent of the time in cities of fewer than 100,000. Nonofficials are found in greater numbers as heads of pyramidal and multipyramidal structures in cities with fewer than 100,000. There are sixteen cases. On a proportionate basis, the number is not great. The stereotype of a pyramid of economic dominants is difficult to maintain in the presence of evidence that most pyramidal structures are not headed by informals.[37]

Population Size and Participation in Power Structure

Scoble suggests that the size of place be controlled for locating differences between leaders and nonleaders. *Hypothesis: The larger the population size, the greater is the participation of politicians in carrying out community political functions: obversely . . . smaller . . . informals.*

36. Compare Gilbert, "Community Power Structure," pp. 53–54.
37. See ibid., pp. 59–60, and Gilbert, "Communities, Power Structures, and Research Bias."

Results: The relationship between size and participation, or leadership, is supported. Population size shares systematic biases with some measures of leadership; when data quality control is applied, the proportion changes for various participants for different population sizes, but the direction of the association does not change.

A nonlinear relationship between population size and participation of various games in the power structure is uncovered in the course of analysis. The overall relationship is as predicted and as shown.[38]

Population Size and Conflict

Clark offers two hypotheses from which a prediction is deduced: (1) the greater the density of cross-cutting status-sets, the more controlled the community conflicts, and (2) the larger the community, the less dense the cross-cutting status-sets (pp. 123–24). *Hypothesis: The larger the community, the less controlled the community conflicts.*

Results: The hypothesis is supported, although the evidence (which is not presented) is biased. Very large cities (over 500,000) tend to have a higher level of conflict than do other cities. Cities under 100,000 population tend to be among those that have no overt conflict.

Population Size and Local Political Parties

A hypothesis from Scoble's list is: *The larger the size of the community, the greater the roles of interest groups and of political parties in policy-making* (p. 118).

Results: Although evidence is not presented (because it is not quality controlled), it partially supports and partially contradicts the prediction. The Democratic Party tends to be dominant in cities of over 500,000. In cities of over 100,000 population, one political party tends to dominate, more often the Democratic than the Republican, but no differences are found for strength of politicians.

In comparing cities over 20,000 with those under 20,000, for the larger it is found that politicians tend to be weak or lack control completely, or they are strong on some issues but weak on others. For the smaller, politicians tend to be strong, balanced, or tend to

38. See "Community Power Structure," p. 54, or "Communities, Power Structures, and Research Bias."

be in a coalition with others. No differences are found in party domination (both, one, or neither dominate) for cities dichotomized at a population size of 20,000.

Population Size and Institutions and Organizations

Population size might be a factor in predicting the importance of institutional and organizational sectors. Scoble predicts the greater role of interest groups in larger cities. Richard Laskin and Serena Phillett recently studied voluntary associational leadership in relation to population size. They investigated four towns, populations 550, 1,050, 2,750, and 4,250. (These would have all been classified as very small in the current study.)

TABLE 2–20. Institutional and Organizational Sectors Tend to be Strong in Large Cities and Weak in Small Cities

	#82 Control of local policies by institutional and organizational sectors is	
	Strong, or moderate	Weak
#23 Population size is		
Medium, small, or very small	47% (48)	79% (11)
Very large, or large	53% (54)	21% (3) P = 0.043

They found, "Whatever criteria are used to identify the reputational influential and the formal leader operationally, it is not possible to conclude that in a given type of community (e.g., the small town) the formal voluntary groups will contribute in some predictable way to the local influence structures."[39]

Variation in control of local policy by institutional sectors is located for different size cities, showing that control tends to be weaker in small cities (see Table 2–20). Seventy-nine per cent of the cities with weak organizational and institutional sectors are very small to medium, whereas only 47 per cent of the cities with strong or moderately strong sectors are very small to medium in size. Characteristics other than size can help explain why, within a given size (e.g., very small towns), the contribution of voluntary groups cannot be predicted. In exploring data, organizations and institutions tend to be stronger in the North Central and West (rather than South and Northeast) and among metropolitan regions which are

39. "An Integrative Analysis of Voluntary Associational Leadership and Reputational Influence," *Sociological Inquiry* 35 (Spring 1965): 185.

growing fast (rather than slow), perhaps reflecting the newness of these regions. For all cities, institutions and organizations tend to be stronger in central cities and in cities where the average education of the population is above the median for the United States.

Population Size and the Function of Local Government and Experts

Hypothesis: "*The larger the size, the greater number of events that become 'issues' . . . the greater the number of public-policy decisions . . . the greater the role of technical expertise as one moves from one decision or scope to another.*"[40]

TABLE 2–21. GOVERNMENT OFFICIALS AND THEIR AGENCIES ARE LEAST IMPORTANT IN ENFORCING INNOVATION IN VERY SMALL CITIES

	#125 Innovation is enforced by		
	Government officials and their agencies	Pressure groups, the electorate, informals, or various segments depending on the issues	
#26 Population size is			
Very small	6% (3)	19% (12)	
Very large, large, medium, or small	94% (49)	81% (51)	P = 0.050

Results: If enforcement of innovation by government officials and their agencies can be accepted as a measure of the role of technical expertise, the hypothesis is supported by evidence in Table 2–21 insofar as very small cities tend less to have officials enforcing innovation than do other cities. Three of fifteen very small cities have enforcement of innovation by government officials and their agencies. The comparable figure for other cities is 49 of 100.

A related idea appears in Banfield and Wilson. The function of politics in the small town is less to resolve issues than to suppress them, to enable people to get along with each other while living together in very close contact. In sizable cities, of course, this need does not exist (p. 25). *Hypothesis: Sizable cities are more likely to handle issues politically (rather than by suppressing them) and therefore are more likely to have the political rather than the good government function.*

Results: The hypothesis is supported. Two population dichot-

40. Scoble, p. 123.

omies are offered in Table 2–22, showing the tendency of smaller cities to have the good government function.

TABLE 2–22. THE LARGER THE CITY, THE MORE IT TENDS TO HAVE THE POLITICAL FUNCTION

	#75 Local government is oriented toward		
	Good government	Mixed good government and machine politics, or machine politics	
Population size is			
#22			
Very large	15% (10)	29% (17)	
Large, medium, small, or very small	85% (57)	71% (42)	P = 0.081
#24			
Very large, large, or medium	69% (46)	85% (50)	
Small, or very small	31% (21)	15% (9)	P = 0.038

Rate of Population Growth and Power Structure

Neither Agger et al. nor Walton find rate of community growth related to power structure.[41] Barth obtained different results: "The rate of growth of the population base of a community is related to the shape of the community influence system. Other things being equal, the more rapid the rate of growth, the more diffuse will be the distribution of community influence" (p. 58).

Results of the current research are contradictory to those of other research: Rate of population growth is negatively associated with diffuse power structure (ecology of games) and positively associated with concentrated power structure (see Table 2–23). If we look at those cities that have had the highest growth rates, we note that none of them have an "ecology of games" power structure, the most diffuse measure in this study. Twenty-one per cent of other cities do have an ecology of games power structure. On one measure of concentrated structure, "pyramid," we find that 64 per cent of cities with high or moderately high growth rates are so characterized, compared to 42 per cent of other cities. It may be that Agger and Walton did not find high growth rates

41. Robert Agger, Daniel Goldrich, and Bert Swanson, *The Rulers and the Ruled* (New York: John Wiley & Sons, 1964), cited as Agger et al.; Walton, "Substance and Artifact."

associated with concentrated or diffuse power structures because their samples were not large enough to scale growth rates.

Table 2–23 also shows that factional structures are all found in the cities with moderate to high growth rates, representing 10 per cent of these growing cities. Cities with low or negative growth rates never are reported as having factional structures.

Growth, Participation, and Issues

The following quotation is from Donald A. Clelland's comparison of "Wheelsburg" to Schulze's study of "Cibola": "It seems more probable that the ED's abnegation of civic responsibility and accountability in Cibola is closely related to the fact that extremely rapid growth and economic fluctuations have generated controversial issues in the community such as are less likely to arise in gradually expanding cities like Wheelsburg."[42] *Hypothesis: Rapid growth leads to controversial issues and subsequent withdrawal of economic dominants from participation in community decision-making.*

Results: Data do not support the hypothesis. No association is found between cities of varying degrees of conflict and the proportion of them that have participation of economic dominants. In cities of various growth rates, no difference is found in participation of economic dominants. Between growth and conflict, one cross-classification reaches alpha: 52 per cent of cities with negative growth rates have medium high or high levels of conflict, whereas 34 per cent of stable or growing cities are so characterized. "The findings in these cities once again point up the need for further comparative research. City *size, economic* history, city *function* and *type of issues* could be systematically examined in order to gain a better understanding of the differences in nature and extent of ED involvement in local power structures" (p. 14).

In order to learn more about the relationship of various types of issues, participation of economic dominants in community power, and other community features, I examined a large number of cross-classifications of these variables. The overwhelming majority of all cities are those whose major decisions are at least partially publicly legitimated. This tendency is greatest when the leaders are not ex-

42. "Economic Dominance and Community Power Structure in a Middle-Sized City," paper delivered at the Ohio Valley Sociological Society meetings, East Lansing, Michigan, 1962, p. 14.

clusively officials. An interpretation is that when decisions are carried out by leaders who are exclusively political figures, many decisions are routine or do not require legitimation. In a minority of cases, officials do carry out policy against the public wishes, but this occurs infrequently. In cities of very high growth rates, community decisions tend less to be publicly legitimated than in cities whose growth rates are moderately high, moderate, low, or negative. The role of economic dominants appears statistically irrelevant in regard to the publicly legitimated nature of issues.

TABLE 2-23. POPULATION GROWTH RATE IS POSITIVELY ASSOCIATED WITH CONCENTRATED AND FACTIONAL POWER STRUCTURES

	Population growth rate is		
	#27 High	#27 Moderately high, moderate, low, or negative	
#89 Top decision-makers are			
An ecology of games	0% (0)	21% (25)	
Not an ecology of games	100% (20)	79% (92)	P = 0.024
	#28 High, or moderately high	#28 Moderate, low, or negative	
#84 Decision-making structure is			
Not a single pyramid	36% (19)	58% (48)	
A single pyramid	64% (33)	42% (34)	P = 0.014
	#29 High, moderately high, or moderate	#29 Low, or negative	
#86 Decision-making structure is			
Not permanent factions	90% (89)	100% (35)	
Permanent factions	10% (10)	0% (0)	P = 0.063

I also examined the nature of leadership and other community variables in relation to the private or public nature of decisions in the community. Private decisions, of course, refer to nongovernmental decisions, such as in the case of privately supported welfare. In communities whose decisions are of a private nature, nonofficials, informals, and economic dominants tend to be the decision-makers; however, these particular findings are based upon measurements which contain systematic error and, thus, are suspect. Additional, unbiased evidence shows that cities in which the leaders decide private issues exclusively tend to be cities characterized by dominance of few industries, or cities whose functional speciality is not in finance or manufacturing (Nelson's classification as described in note 28 of this chapter). One further tendency found for cities whose decisions are in the private realm is that 83 per cent of them have moderate, low, or negative growth rates, rather than high or moderately high rates. The total number of cities whose decisions are in the private realm exclusively is not large, amounting to only 14 of 143 on which such data are available.

Of 143 cities, 94 have leaders who decide issues in the public realm exclusively. Among metropolitan central cities, decisions tend more to be in the public realm in functional metropolises rather than in the partial metropolises, subcenters, and so on. Cities whose decisions are in the public realm exclusively also tend to be economically diversified and tend to be those other than the most rapidly growing cities. Elected officials and politicians tend to be key figures. Informals, nonofficials, and economic dominants tend to be of minimal importance in cities whose major decisions are in the public arena exclusively.

6. REGIONAL GROUPING

Agger et al. say that it is generally assumed that regional differences play a significant part in the structure and functioning of community politics (p. 125). Walton includes the following hypothesis in his inventory: "Regional differences obtain." He reports that the hypothesis is not clearly supported although data show tendencies in that direction: regional differences are somewhat clearer in the Northeast and North Central regions, reflecting less concentration of power than is found in the South (p. 435). Scoble attempts to explain regional differences: "The general trend of the regional economy may be exceedingly important . . . the economy of the South . . . is now going through one of the economic-growth states that W. W. Rostow has pointed out—we might say it is at the 'take-off' stage. The economy of New England, on the other hand, has been depressed ever since the end of World War II and has been going through a very slow and very painful readjustment. . . . One might perhaps explain the observed differences in the roles, say, of inherited wealth, by the greater staying power and residue of 'traditionalism' in the South. . . . In such a situation, it may be that the bankers, owners of the locally controlled businesses, and so on, are the men who make all effective decisions in the community" (pp. 119–20).

TABLE 2–24. A COMPARISON OF CITIES IN THE SOUTH WITH
OTHER U.S. CITIES

	#4 Cities located in the		
	South	Northeast, North Central, or West	
#28 Whose population growth rate is			
High or moderately high	71% (29)	23% (23)	
Moderate, low, or negative	29% (12)	77% (77)	P = 0.000
#31 Those whose median income is			
Below the U.S. median	74% (26)	14% (10)	
Above the U.S. median	26% (9)	86% (60)	P = 0.000
#34 Unemployment rate at the time of study is			
Low or average	71% (25)	53% (37)	
High	29% (10)	47% (33)	P = 0.092
#45 Median age for census year is			
Young	89% (25)	32% (22)	
Old	11% (3)	68% (46)	P = 0.000
#62 Local elections are			
Nonpartisan	76% (19)	50% (40)	
National party tickets	24% (6)	50% (40)	P = 0.036
#63 Local electoral system is			
At-large	74% (17)	44% (28)	
Ward	26% (6)	56% (35)	P = 0.027
#66 Local government is			
City-manager form	68% (23)	34% (31)	
Not city-manager form	32% (11)	66% (60)	P = 0.001
#80 Government experts primarily			
Suggest policy	83% (10)	52% (15)	
Legitimate policy	17% (2)	48% (14)	P = 0.084
#92 Top decision-makers are			
An elite or quasi-elite	50% (19)	32% (30)	
A weak elite, weak quasi-elite, or an ecology of games	50% (19)	68% (64)	P = 0.073
#96 Entry into local policy-making is			
Open to persons of high SES or middle-class Anglos	75% (15)	55% (43)	
Almost completely open, or open to ethnics	25% (5)	45% (35)	P = 0.131

Data from the current inquiry do not support the idea that the role of economically dominant persons is more important in the South than in other areas, but other ideas do gain support. In comparing the South to the Northeast, North Central, and West, differences are found in economic and political structural variables (see Table 2–24, not data quality controlled). Nearly identical results are found when the subregions South Atlantic and East South Central are contrasted to the subregion New England.

Starting at the top of Table 2–24 we observe that population growth rates are significantly higher in the South than elsewhere. In the Northeast, North Central, or West, 77 per cent of the cities were moderate, low, or negative in their growth rates and 23 per cent were high or moderately high. In the South, almost the opposite picture obtained: only 29 per cent of cities were moderate to negative in growth rates and 71 per cent were high or moderately high.

Median incomes in the South tended to be below the median for the United States. Seventy-four per cent of cities in the South were below this average income, but only 14 per cent of other cities fell below the U.S. median. Despite the relatively low income levels in the South, unemployment rates were not high. In fact, 71 per cent of southern cities were low or average in their unemployment rates and 29 per cent were high. Among the other cities, 53 per cent fell into the low or average unemployment rates classification, and 47 per cent were high.

Population in the South is, on the average, younger than for the United States as a whole. Eighty-nine per cent of the southern cities in the study have median population ages that are below the U.S. median, whereas 32 per cent of cities outside of the South do.

Local elections in the southern sample tend to be nonpartisan and at-large, and local governments tend to take the city-manager form. While 50 per cent of cities in the Northeast, North Central, or West have nonpartisan elections (rather than elections on national party tickets), 76 per cent of cities in the South have nonpartisan elections. Outside of the South, 44 per cent of cities have at-large rather than ward local elections, while 74 per cent of the southern cities have an at-large form. Finally, 34 per cent of nonsouthern cities have the city-manager form, while 68 per cent of the southern cities do.

Continuing to follow Table 2–24, we find that in the South, government experts tend more to suggest rather than legitimate policy. Eighty-three per cent of southern cities have experts in the role of suggesting policy, whereas such a tendency is found in other cities about half of the time. We might speculate that places with relatively rapid growth are characterized by innovation coming from experts, in comparison to more stable places such as New England.

Power structures tend to be somewhat concentrated in the South, as Walton found. Half of the cities in the southern group have an elite or a quasi-elite structure, whereas 32 per cent of cities outside the South do. While half of the southern cities have a less concentrated structure, 68 per cent of the other cities do. A difference appears in the relative ease of entry into these structures, supporting Scoble's ideas: in 75 per cent of the southern cities in the sample, if power structures are open, they are open to persons of high socioeconomic status or to middle-class Anglos, whereas in the remainder of the nation, 45 per cent of the open structures are relatively open to all social types in the community or to a particular ethnic group. This might be explained, as Scoble suggests, by the greater relative poverty of the average person in the South.

7. CITY TYPE

Previous research demonstrates the importance of city type as a predictive variable for power structure.

City Type and Power Structure

Type of city is associated with power structures as follows: central cities in metropolitan regions are at the "diffused influence extreme."[43] Schulze signifies the importance of "central city, satellite, and suburb," for power structure and processes.[44] If nonmetropolitan areas might be viewed as having the least degree of differentiation of the polity from the kinship and economic systems, then Rogers' notion is useful: areas with a high degree of differentiation (i.e., metropolitan) are associated with more pluralistic political systems (p. 47). In an empirical analysis of two cities, Presthus finds partial support for a related hypothesis originally offered by Lane: "The better organized a social stratum (class, ethnic group, residential area) under its own leadership, the more politically effec-

43. Mann, p. 62.
44. Quoted in Miller, "Democracy and Decision Making," p. 62.

tive it will be. . . . ·Metropolitan areas offer greater opportunities for pluralistic patterns than smaller communities" (p. 415). *Hypothesis: The less the city resembles a metropolitan center, the more it tends to have a concentrated power structure; obversely . . . more central . . . pluralistic.*

Results: The hypothesis is supported. The author has tested the hypothesis elsewhere.[45]

> The greatest proportion of pyramidal structures are found in independent cities. The largest proportion of multipyramidal structures are found in industrial suburbs. A fluid power structure occurs most frequently, on a proportionate basis, in metropolitan central cities, and the residential suburb is the most likely place to locate a factional structure. 'Other,' usually representing a situation in flux or nonclassifiable for other reasons, is most often found in rural villages or trade centers.
>
> Proportionately, a group of any kind (elite, weak elite, or group with amount of control not known) is most frequently found in residential suburbs and independent cities. Aggregates of leaders who do not form a group (quasi-elite, weak quasi-elite, or aggregate) are most often found in industrial suburbs and trade centers. An ecology of games is most probably found in central cities (p. 60).

I concluded that while economic function of a city best predicts the role of officials and informals in policy-making, the type of city is the best predictor of the form of power structure.

City Type and Participation in Decision-Making

In earlier analysis, *it was hypothesized that the less central the city, the more likely informals are important for carrying out community political functions; obversely . . . more central . . . politicians.*

The *results* were weak. A slight tendency was found for informals to be leaders outside of metropolitan central cities.[46] Further analysis indicates that informals are relatively important in rural areas. Participation from all sectors, when it occurs, takes place in the central city.

45. "Community Power Structure," pp. 54–55.
46. Ibid., p. 55.

City Type, Issues, and Conflicts

On the basis of data not published here, it can be said that metropolitan central cities tend not to be among those cities having no conflict at all. Levels of conflict tend to be higher for industrial rather than residential suburbs and for rural farm rather than rural trade areas.

In trying to understand the kinds of issues that are important in central cities, it is found that (as might be expected) the decisions of power groups tend more to be in the public realm exclusively in central cities. This tendency is not very strong (see Table 2–25). A larger percentage of central cities have leaders whose decisions are in the public realm exclusively. Population density is also used as a measure of "centrality of city," with the denser population taken as being more central. Fewer of the less dense cities have public realm decisions only, as shown in Table 2–25.

TABLE 2–25. ISSUES DECIDED BY POWER GROUP TEND TO BE IN THE PUBLIC REALM EXCLUSIVELY IN METROPOLITAN CENTRAL CITIES

	#114 Power groups decisions are		
	In the public realm exclusively	Other than in the public realm exclusively	
#8 Present character is			
Not metropolitan central	37% (34)	51% (24)	
Metropolitan central	63% (57)	49% (23)	P = 0.147
#21 Population per square mile is			
Less than 5,000	32% (12)	59% (10)	
5,000 or more	68% (25)	41% (7)	P = 0.081

8. CONSTITUTIONAL STRUCTURE

The final group of hypotheses used as independent variables concern the constitutional structure of local government. These local governmental variables include the electoral system, council or commission form, and manager or non-manager form. Robert L. Crain and Donald B. Rosenthal find governmental forms (mayor-council, commission, and manager) and electoral systems (partisan, non-partisan) are related to the handling of fluoridation issues[47] (see

47. "Structure and Values in Local Political Systems: The Case of Fluoridation Decisions," *Journal of Politics* 28 (February 1966): 169–95.

Table 2–26). The top of the table shows that, although there are few high conflict cases, all of them occur in ward electoral systems and where governments are not city-manager form. The lower portion of the table shows that cities having commission form of government appear to have relatively low levels of conflict. Eleven per cent of cities with medium low or low conflict are commission form, and 2 per cent of cities with high or medium conflict are commission form. Also, 49 per cent of cities with medium low or low conflict are city-manager form while 35 per cent of

TABLE 2–26. Conflict Is Related to Constitutional Form of Local Government

	Degree of community conflict is		
	#98 High	#98 Medium, medium low, or low	
#63 Local electoral system is			
At-large	0% (0)	58% (45)	
Ward	100% (3)	42% (33)	P = 0.084
#66 Local government is			
City-manager form	0% (0)	45% (51)	
Not city-manager form	100% (4)	55% (62)	P = 0.131
	#99 High or medium	#99 Medium low, or low	
#65 Form of local government is			
Commission	2% (1)	11% (8)	
Mayor-council. town meeting, or mixed council commission	98% (46)	89% (64)	P = 0.086
#66 Local government is			
City-manager form	35% (16)	49% (35)	
Not city-manager form	65% (30)	51% (36)	P = 0.132

cities with high or medium conflict are city-manager form (the latter all being "medium" conflict since the upper part of the table shows no "high" for manager cities).

Constitutional Form and Power Structure

Here is a pair of *hypotheses* that appear contradictory: (1) *The larger the number of governmental statuses in a community filled according to nonpartisan electoral procedures, the more monolithic the power structure.*[48] (2) *Nonpartisan elections are personality*

48. Clark, p. 125.

*based and partisan elections are issue based. Politics is more un-
structured in nonpartisan cities, with the only election issue re-
tention or dismissal of the manager.*[49]

Results: Data support the notion that cities with nonpartisan elections tend to be less concentrated in power structure. Scoble suggests as the first political variable that should engage our attention
the governmental form (strong or weak mayor-council system,
council-manager plan, and commission form): "Although we *think*
these may be important, we really don't know because no one has
studied form of government systematically and comparatively. We
don't even know whether the strong and weak mayor systems are
only 'pure types.' . . . Other forms of municipal government
may be of importance for the types of decision-making patterns
that occur. As one illustration, a commission . . . tends to result,
according to Adrian, in some sort of the bargaining system among
equals. . . . One could hypothesize that the governmental structure is important for the pattern of decision-making that results"
(pp. 120–21). Finally, Walton found no significant relationship between type of city government and power structure (note 18).

Governmental form has the following measures in the current
inquiry: ward–at-large electoral system; partisan-nonpartisan electoral system; mayor-council-commission forms; and city manager–
not city manager. Mayor-council form has no power structure correlates, nor does commission form.

Ward systems tend more to be fluid in structure than do at-large
systems (see Table 2–27). Twenty-nine per cent of ward and 13
per cent of at-large cities have the most pluralistic power structure,
an "ecology of games." City-manager cities tend more to have factional structures and tend less to be pluralistic in power structure
than do cities without managers. Seventeen per cent of city-manager
cities and 3 per cent of other cities have decision-making structures
marked by permanent factions. Eighty-nine per cent of city-manager cities are less pluralistic than an "ecology of games," and 74
per cent of other cities are equally less pluralistic, as shown in the
table. We know that the manager form, at-large elections, and nonpartisanship tend to go together. It can be guessed that even though
the constitutional structure is "objective" and treated as an independent variable, it is causally related to other features of a city

49. Kammerer and DeGrove, *Florida City Managers*, pp. 31–32.

(such as centrality, region, rate of growth, and population characteristics).

Nonpartisanship and Local Political Parties

Charles R. Adrian believes that nonpartisanship weakens political
parties.[50] Scoble explains why:

> We think that there is an important difference between non-
> partisan and partisan elections. From all we know, nonpartisan
> elections usually also take the "at large" form, and this in
> turn normally makes it easier for high-voting-rate (equals
> middle- and upper-class) "wards" to dominate the legisla-
> ture. The nonpartisan electoral scheme normally depresses the
> effective role of political parties and of working-class interest
> groups—as was intended by the Progressive reformers. . . .
>
> It is relevant to question whether the local party system is
> one-part Republican, one-part Democrat or a competitive sys-
> tem in which both parties can share realistic hopes for win-
> ning elections. Each pattern is both a cause and a reflection
> of differing political styles in local policy-making; at least,
> these categories direct our attention to a . . . political factor
> (pp. 121–22).

TABLE 2–27. WARD ELECTIONS TEND MORE AND CITY MANAGER FORMS TEND
LESS TO RESULT IN ECOLOGICAL POWER STRUCTURES—FACTIONAL
STRUCTURES TEND TO BE MORE COMMON IN MANAGER CITIES

	#63 Local election system is		
	Ward	At-large	
#89 Top decision-makers are			
Not an ecology of games	71% (27)	87% (39)	
An ecology of games	29% (11)	13% (6)	P = 0.104

	#65 Local government is		
	City-manager form	Not city-manager form	
#89 Top decision-makers are			
An ecology of games	11% (6)	26% (18)	
Not an ecology of games	89% (47)	74% (51)	P = 0.065
#86 Decision-making structure is			
Not permanent factions	83% (44)	97% (67)	
Permanent factions	17% (9)	3% (2)	P = 0.010

50. "Some General Characteristics of Nonpartisan Elections," *American
Political Science Review* 46 (September 1952): 766–76.

Adrian and Scoble are supported by data summarized in Table 2–28 (which is not data quality controlled). (For cities with at-large elections, we have similar findings as for nonpartisan cities.) Table 2–28 summarizes many tables concerned with nonpartisan local elections, similar findings obtain as do for nonpartisan cities.) Table absence of control by politicians. Sixty-seven per cent of cities with nonpartisan local elections also have at-large elections, 67 per cent of cities whose policy is not dominated by major political parties have at-large elections, and 76 per cent of cities whose politicians are weak in controlling local policy have at-large elections.

By reading down the columns, we see that in cities with nonpartisan local elections, structures are mostly headed by combinations of nonofficials and officials, and participation comes from politicians, business, and interest groups. Neither political party dominates in 92 per cent of nonpartisan cities. On the average, politicians and party are weaker in nonpartisan systems. Fifty-nine

TABLE 2–28. CHARACTERISTICS ASSOCIATED WITH NONPARTISAN ELECTIONS, LACK OF PARTY DOMINATION, AND CONTROL OF LOCAL POLICIES BY POLITICIANS

	#62 Nonpartisan local elections	#68 Local policy dominated by neither major political party	#72 Control of policies by politicians and party is absent or weak
At-large elections	67%	67%	76%
Who heads structure?	Mostly combination of non-officials and officials	Mostly officials and nonofficials	Varies: Nonofficials 19% Officials 58%
Who participates?	Politicians, business, interest groups, etc.	Politicians and others	54% informals, all economic dominants; 8% politicians only
Which party dominates?	92% neither political party	100% neither party (redundancy)	86% neither party
How much control have politicians and party?	On the average, weaker than in partisan systems	On the average, weaker than in cities dominated by one or both parties	100% no control or some control (redundancy)
Other traits?	59% have manager 17% suburban 46% high or moderately high growth rates	54% have manager 15% suburban 45% high or moderately high growth rates 83% nonpartisan	No differences in manager; approximately 80% are central cities No differences in growth rates 76% nonpartisan

per cent of nonpartisan towns have a city manager, 17 per cent are suburban, and 46 per cent have high or moderately high growth rates.

Cities whose policies are not dominated by either major political party have structures that are headed by both officials and non-officials, and participation is from politicians and others. Politicians and their parties are weaker on the average than in cities whose policies are dominated by one or both parties. Fifty-four per cent of cities which are not dominated by parties have city managers, 15 per cent are suburbs, 45 per cent have high or moderately high growth rates, and 83 per cent have nonpartisan elections.

Finally, in regard to cities whose control of policies by politicians and party is weak or entirely absent, we find all of the following characteristics. Nineteen per cent of them are headed by non-officials and 58 per cent of them are headed by officials, so the pattern here is more variable than found among the other types (variables 62 and 68 in Table 2–28). Participation in 54 per cent of these cities is from informals, all of whom are economic dominants, and 8 per cent of these cities have participation from politicians only. Again, the pattern is more variable than for the preceding columns. Where control by politicians is absent or weak, in 86 per cent of these cities neither political party dominates. No differences are found in proportions which have city managers or in growth rates. About 80 per cent of these are central cities and 76 per cent of them are nonpartisan in electoral structure.

Nonpartisanship and Suburbs

Robert C. Wood says the expert in the suburbs is entrusted with the tough problems while the suburban man grows apolitical. This is because of his cloak of nonpartisanship and the impossibility of keeping himself informed about every complex issue. Wood sees the suburban government as one which is run by "automation" and, under these circumstances, "the purest theory of democracy requires no democratic action of responsibility at all."[51] *Hypothesis: Nonpartisan towns and suburbs tend to have experts initiating (suggesting) policy rather than legitimating it.*

Results: There is no significant relationship between either suburbs or nonpartisanship and the place of experts. One inverse rela-

51. *Suburbia: Its People and Their Politics* (Boston: Houghton Mifflin Co., 1958), p. 197.

tionship is found between nonpartisan towns and innovation being enforced by government officials and their agencies. (This supports Crain's findings on fluoridation adoption.)

Constitutional Structure and Participation of the Population

Adrian suggests that nonpartisanship tends to frustrate protest voting. Cities which hold nonpartisan local elections and those running candidates on party tickets were compared to see if there is a difference in the political place and strength of the population, but no differences are found.

9. OUTLOOKS, VALUES, AND PERCEPTIONS

Unfortunately, no measure of outlooks, values, or perceptions of the leaders or of the led have been included in this study. An important and relatively unexplored area is the relation of outlooks toward the realities of politics. What is the actual relationship between perceiving influentials or an elite and the actual functions performed by them?[52] The question cannot be answered in the framework of this inquiry.

Clark suggests "the more paternalistic the value system of elite groups in the community, the greater their involvement in community affairs" (p. 125). Banfield and Wilson emphasize the tendency of members of different social categories to be different in ethos: Protestants and upper-middle and upper classes tend to be public-regarding. Members of the lower-middle class tend to be private-regarding. People who are decidedly private- or public-regarding tend to be so on all matters: "Decidedly public-regarding and decidedly private-regarding voters tend to be further apart on all matters, including those which have no public-private dimension, than are other voters" (p. 235).

William H. Form and Warren L. Sauer investigated labor's image of the power structure:

> Labor perceives the community power structure as composed primarily of an integrated management clique which controls the outcome of most significant community issues.
>
> Variations in labor's image of its community power are accounted for by the age, community involvement, union po-

52. One approach is given by Orrin Klapp, *Symbolic Leaders* (Chicago: Aldine Press, 1964).

sition, and degree of influence among union personnel. Older ex–A.F.L. union leaders, those who hold high offices and have great influence in the union perceive the local power structure as less business dominated than the younger unionists, ex–C.I.O. officials, those who hold lower union posts, and those who have less influence in union circles.[53]

James McKee, also concerned with labor's image and identification, points out that according to the Marxians, the result of a working-class group becoming class conscious should be a radical overturning of society: the new class takes over power, and the old classes recede. But no such development has accompanied the rise of labor in Steelport. Labor's rise to power may "be accompanied by an identification with the community, and the conflict may diminish greatly when labor's participation in community decision-making is legitimized."[54]

My impression is that we need to know more about how various members of a community view the power structure and whether or not these views have any important consequences for the sociopolitical system.

53. "Organized Labor's Image of Community Power Structure," *Social Forces* 38 (May 1960): 334.
54. "The Power to Decide," in Meyer Weinberg and Oscar Shabet, eds., *Society and Man* (Englewood Cliffs, N.J.: Prentice Hall, 1956), p. 538.

3. The Development of Community Power Theory

THE PURPOSE of this study was to test systematically the large number of hypotheses from community power studies with data other than those upon which they were based.

The findings are presented here with the hope that they and data currently being gathered[1] will enable scholars to build more sophisticated models, or even middle-range theories, relating to American community power.

To share my experience toward this goal, I bring together the preceding material in summary form and report some insights and theory which evolved during the study.

To do this, I shall share some of the operating assumptions of the study and indicate how they stood up in the light of experience. (1) One assumption at the outset was that the differences in research findings of community power studies were due either to real underlying community differences or to biased research theories and methods. (2) A second was that the various hypotheses about community power (such as the larger the community, the more pluralistic the power structure) could be brought together and formed into an internally consistent set of axiomatic hypotheses. (3) Still another and related assumption was that from this research, a theory would emerge at least at minimal level, i.e., a string of accepted hypotheses could be presented. Finally, (4) nation-state was a control variable from the beginning, on the assumption that it was something that ought to be controlled.

Before I report on how these assumptions fared, I should like to indicate a general limit of political studies at the local level. Douglas Fox deals with it in "Whither Community Power

1. See Peter H. Rossi and Robert L. Crain, "The NORC Permanent Community Sample," *Public Opinion Quarterly* 32 (Summer 1968): 261–72.

Studies?"[2] He concludes that some large proportion of the decision-making process which affects the local territorial grouping is actually carried out at state and national levels. He suggests that research resources may be used to better advance our knowledge by including studies of state and national policy-making. I might also add that there is an increased emphasis today on the study of policy outcomes, with power structures often conceived as an intervening variable. There is today a desire to find fresh ways of dealing with power studies.

1.

Returning to this study, one major conclusion that I came to regarding community power studies is that despite all kinds of random and systematic biases, the underlying community differences forced the variety of research findings.[3] A dramatic demonstration of this occurs when we examine the results that have been obtained by practitioners of different disciplines. Sociologists have much more often found "informals" as the decision-makers, whereas members of other disciplines more often found officials, politicians, and / or others in key spots. If we then group studies according to the discipline of the researchers and analyze each group separately, we find that the relationship between type of leadership and size of the community's population continues to exist. A detailed report can be found.[4] In short, in community power studies, any particular study may be unreliable, but, as a group, these can be quality controlled and analyzed. Treated as groups of reports, trustworthy political differences are found among cities of different types, functions, social characteristics, and so on.

2.

Another conclusion I was forced to by the experience of this research is that while an axiomatic theory of community power structures is logically possible, it simply did not prove apt as a map of empirical reality.

A pilot study was conducted during the course of gathering data. About one-fourth of the cities from the total sample were

2. *Polity* 3 (Summer 1971): 576–85.
3. Gilbert, "Communities, Power Structures, and Research Bias."
4. Ibid.

included. Individual plausible hypotheses were tested. Some were suggested by the literature, others were hunches. Among the hypotheses that were supported, some were selected for inclusion in an axiomatic system. Inclusion was determined by theoretical relevance of the variables and logical consistency of relationships between them.

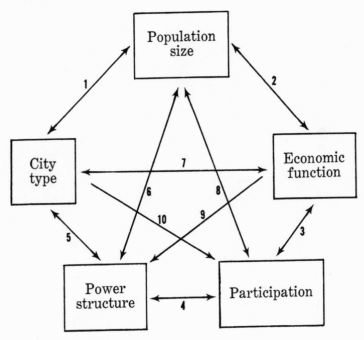

TABLE 3–1. Ten Logical Axiomatic Relationships among Five Community Variables

Five variables were finally included in the axiomatic theory: (1) size of community population, (2) economic base of community, (3) type of city (central city in SMSA, residential or industrial suburb in an SMSA, independent city, rural village, and trade center), (4) power structure concentration or diffusion, and (5) types of leadership. Each variable appeared with all others in pairs to form ten interrelated hypotheses. Table 3–1 has a diagrammatic schema.

I did not find any single theoretical or empirical study that could be used as a basis for this work. No theory was specific enough to allow the deduction of interrelated hypotheses. No generalizations brought together all of the ideas which exist on the topic. A framework could be built from existing orientations to data but would not provide testable hypotheses. I finally combined general orientations provided by sociology and political science with specific hypotheses developed from research.

The texture of urban life was the concern of the sociologist Louis Wirth:

> An industrial city will differ significantly in social respects from a commercial, mining, fishing, resort, university, and capital city. A one-industry city will present different sets of social characteristics from a multi-industry city as will an industrially balanced from an imbalanced city, a suburb from a satellite, a residential suburb from an industrial suburb, a city within a metropolitan region from one lying outside, an old city from a new one, a Southern city from a New England, a Middle-Western from a Pacific Coast city, a growing from a stable and from a dying city.
>
> Presumably some of the characteristics of cities are more significant in conditioning the nature of urban life than others, and we may expect the outstanding features of the urban-social scene to vary in accordance with the size, density, and differences in the functional type of cities.[5]

These characteristics are also significant for political life. Their value to power structure analysis is not immediately apparent, however, and cannot be derived from the work of Wirth.

A complementary but different view of the city is offered by the political scientist Norton Long. He says that for many purposes, there is no overall organization in the metropolitan community. Yet, decisions are made and carried out by a process which Long calls an "ecology of games."[6] In his conception, "games" in the local community include banking, contracting, newspaper production, ecclesiastics, politics, and civic leadership. A game is a serious activity and is characterized by the following: (1) rules (these are equivalent to norms of conduct, and are intrinsic to all social activity); (2) goals (the goal is an end, purpose, or aim of a game); and (3) score-keeping (the performance

5. "Urbanism as a Way of Life."
6. *The Polity* (Chicago: Rand McNally and Co., 1962), pp. 139–55.

of each player is evaluated according to his degree of conformity to the rules of the game and whether he achieves a desired goal).

Cooperation among games is possible in a territorial community because a general definition of success is shared among the various games. In their individual pursuits, players of different games mesh and thus bring about overall results in the territorial system. According to Long, cooperation among the games is "ecological" and not rational. Overall planning and control are absent. Public functions are accomplished by the unintended cooperation of people who are acting to achieve their assorted goals.[7] "The process of accomplishing public functions" can be translated to "the structure of power" in order to conceptualize the variables implicit in Long's work. (1) Instead of seeing decision-making and the carrying out of political activities as absolutely ecological processes in the territorial system, we prefer to conceive of them as ranging between "ecological" and "rational." We can then ask, "To what degree is any structure of power concentrated (rational) or pluralistic (ecological)?" (2) The various "games" in the territorial system are reconceived as "participation or leadership from various sectors," such as economic, political, and civic.

Answers were sought to these questions: (1) Under what set of conditions are public decisions and actions most concentrated or pluralistic? (2) Under what set of conditions do leaders from one or another sector of the local community dominate public decision-making? Wirth's significant characteristics were used as a set of conditions which would underlie variations in structures of power. Though neither Wirth nor Long provided specific relations of the variables, both provided raw material from which hypotheses were constructed.

Relationships of Variables

Although agreement was not complete, previous research did suggest how size, city type, and economic function related to power structures. Hypotheses were deduced or inferred from examining empirical generalizations and other analyses. All of these have been dealt with in the preceding inventory and are found elsewhere.[8] The five variables—population size, city type, economic

7. Ibid., passim.
8. Gilbert, "Community Power Structure"; Clark, pp. 122–25.

function, power structure, and leadership or participation—formed
ten hypotheses by pairing each variable with the remaining ones.[9]
Each hypothesis was tested with data.

Each variable was operationalized in several ways, which per-
mits many tests of each hypothesis. (One hypothesis could be tested
forty-five ways, using five measures of types of leadership and
nine measures of power structure.) With multimeasures of each
concept and many working definitions of each hypothesis, no
concept rested on one measure, and no hypothesis could be supported or ruled out by a single correlation. Bearing this in mind,
it was found that some hypotheses were not supported, some
were weakly supported, and two were strongly supported. When
a hypothesis was supported by most tests of it and there were no
contradictions, the validity of the measures, concepts, and hypotheses were taken as convergent.

One hypothesis proved more than a simple relationship between
two variables and destroyed the axiomatic form. I had proposed
that the more concentrated the power structure, the more likely
leadership is from informals, and the more pluralistic the power
structure, the more likely leadership is from politicians and officials. Examination of a large number of tables in detail revealed
that in fact *the more concentrated the power structure, the more
likely leadership comes from but one sector, either officials or
informals; and the more pluralistic the power structure, the more
likely leadership comes from two or more sectors. If leadership
comes from one sector, which sector it comes from is best determined by the economics of the city.* That is, a second important
finding is that *economics best predicted leadership or participation.*
A third important discovery is that *city type is most important in
predicting shape of the power structure.* Population size, it seems,
gains its importance as a variable because it is correlated with
variables that make a difference—economic function and city type.
These results are summarized in Table 3–2 and will be elaborated
on in this chapter.

3.

By now it is evident that developing empirically based community power theory is not merely a question of stringing together
hypotheses. A further complexity implicit in the above, but even

9. Adapted from Gilbert, "Community Power Structure," p. 61A.

nore evident when examining large correlation matrixes, is that groups of variables are interrelated. An example is that city type correlates with age of population and with constitutional structure. Within the constitutional structure, variables correlate. These include whether elections are organized by ward or are at-large and whether they are partisan or nonpartisan, or whether or not there is a city manager and whether the form of government is commission or council. Features of the constitutional structure additionally correlate with region of the country, rate of population growth, and other population characteristics.

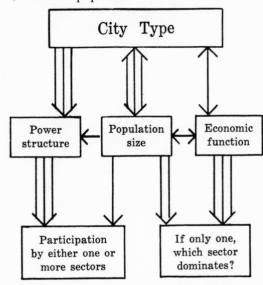

TABLE 3–2. EMPIRICAL RELATIONSHIPS AMONG CITY TYPE, POWER STRUCTURE, ECONOMIC FUNCTION, PARTICIPATION, AND POPULATION SIZE

For all of its correlates, the constitutional structure of the community, often a focus of political research, appears in the current study to be a weak variable overall for predicting features of power structures. (Recent research shows its relevance for policy outcomes.) In summarizing features that are associated, we can say that cities with ward elections tend to have more fluid power structures and more conflict than others. Cities without city managers are less frequently factional in structure than others, are generally more pluralistic than others, and are less likely to have the good government function. Cities with commission

forms of government have lower levels of conflict than other
Finally, nonpartisan cities have weaker political parties and les
concentrated power structures than other cities.

Some power structure variables are associated with each othe
As already indicated, when the power structure is concentratec
leadership tends to be from one area such as politics or busines
If one sector dominates, it is likely to be the politicians, parties, an
officials in large or economically diversified cities. It is probabl
nonofficials in middle-sized to small or one-industry cities. Th
type of people who select candidates for local political offices ten
to be the dominant type in local politics. Good government citie
tend to have less conflict, or the conflict is managed better, tha
in other cities. Political function governments are found in bot
the most monolithic settings and the most pluralistic. In middle
range power structures, we are more likely to find good governmer
or mixed function government.

Although population size is important as an independent var
able because of its concomitance with economic function an
city type, it is nevertheless worthwhile to discuss it. Rate of pop
ulation growth, also strongly associated with many other objec
tive variables, is a good independent variable. Population size
correlated with whether leaders will be governmental officials c
not, although the relationship is not linear. The larger cities ten
to have politicians, and the smaller, informals. But underlying th
distribution of leadership types by population size—and the re:
son size matters for leadership—is the community economi
function. Communities of various economic functional types ten
to cluster around modal sizes.[10]

Conflict is an important correlate of population size. The mo
unmanageable conflicts have been found in the very large citie
Mere numbers, however, are not the cause. Very large cities hav
disproportionate numbers of people who are poor and uned
cated, and are homes of political minorities. These cities are als
"overdiversified" economically in that they are national cente
of finance, manufacturing, communications, and the like. The
are also havens for social deviants who find anonymity in them. An
of course, they are the location of first arrival for immigrants an
in-migrants. All of these features of very large cities in Unite

10. Gilbert, "Communities, Power Structures, and Research Bias."

States society are probably responsible for the greater conflict found in such places.

Very large cities, those of 500,000 or more, also tend more to have fluid power structures. Size is less related to very concentrated structures. Concentrated structures occur at all sizes relatively frequently. If a concentrated structure does appear in cities over 100,000, the important figures are political heads. But, as already mentioned, the relationship between political leadership and size is not linear. Most very small towns studied are led by formally elected political officials. Most of the towns ranging from 20,000 to 50,000 population are dominated by nonpolitical persons or coalitions between such persons and elected officials. Most cities of real size are ruled by people who hold political office, although these cities are frequently fluid in structure.

The larger cities tend to have stress on the political function of government, the smaller cities emphasizing good government. In cities over 500,000, Democrats tend to dominate. In all cities over 100,000, there is a trend for one party to dominate—Republican or Democratic. The actual strength that politicians have (or fail to have) does vary by population size.

Rates of population growth are underexplored here. We do know that cities with negative growth rates tend to have high conflict. (Negative growth rate cities are frequently older, central cities in metropolitan areas.) Cities of very rapid growth rates tend to have, contrary to popular belief, concentrated power structures. As said earlier, growth is a variable that deserves more attention.

City type has proven to be a durable variable in this study. It is a powerful predictor of the relative shape of the power structure. It may prove in the long run that (because of the population's social characteristics associated with city type) city type really gains its power to predict from the population's social characteristics. For example, younger, wealthier, more educated, and nonethnic populations are likely to be found outside of central cities (where politics is of the good government variety). Older, poorer, less educated, and ethnic populations are likely to be found in central cities (where conflict is more likely and governments must perform political functions). Population growth rates and population density are also associated with city type.

The modal type of power structure in central cities in metro-

politan areas is fluid. This structure may vary according to issue
or may be particularly amorphous. The central city is where all sec
tors or many sectors may be involved in policy-making, with
little coordination and rational planning. Independent cities (outside
metropolitan areas) are most often pyramidal in their structure
of power and are likely to have a single group (or even person
at the apex, whether or not the group controls all policies. Indus
trial suburbs in metropolitan areas tend to have unassociated in
dividuals as community decision-makers and several pyramids of
power, a form sometimes called multipyramidal. Residential sub
urbs have a single group (or a factional structure) as a modality
Although there were few cases from which to generalize, I find
that rural villages and trade centers are harder to categorize, with
a tendency to be in a state of flux.

In this study we find that economic function of a city (a vari
able which was originally a simple question, "How do people get
a living?") is most useful in indicating what types of leadership are
likely to be found. Economically diversified cities tend to have
politicians as heads of power structures. Towns with one or a
few industries dominating tend to have business leaders at the
top; rarely do they have only politicians dominant in community
decision-making. Recalling that pluralistic structures tend to have
leadership from both officials and nonofficials, we conclude that
economic function of a city is the best predictor of whether
leaders will be officials or informals when the power structure is
relatively concentrated.

Although economic function of a community is generally un
related to power structure type, some relationships exist. Func
tional metropolises tend to be pluralistic. Specialized cities tend
very strongly to be factional (and never have only nonofficials as
heads).

Social characteristics of the population are influential in politi
cal structure. Some of the associations reviewed show that young
and/or affluent populations tend to have more concentrated
power structures in their communities. (Education here is un
associated.) In communities above average in education or wealth
we find disproportionate domination by nonofficials, lower levels
of conflict, increased participation of citizens, and local govern
ments oriented to good government.

In the long run, historical factors appear to have played a part n current regional differences. The degree of pluralism found in any community seems related to the history of the region. Communities in the West tend to be more pluralistic than those of the East. There is a trend in the United States away from centralized forms of power structures in local communities and toward more pluralistic structures. The increasing scale of our society, or what can be called urbanization in the broadest sense of the term, is the cause.

City governments appear to be decreasingly oriented toward the political function because some cities that were formerly oriented to machine politics are adding good government to their functions.

Data show no relationship between conflict and the time dimension. (These data were based on studies conducted prior to the summer of 1967 when many riots took place in major cities in the United States.)

Structures are decreasingly headed exclusively by officials. An increasing proportion of cities have economic dominants as upper-level power leaders. The increase of economic dominants is misleading, for it reflects changes in smaller cities, those that are dependent on few industries for livelihood. Since the end of World War II, 8 per cent of cities on which we have data have leadership which includes representation from all sectors within the city, or leadership from pressure groups and aldermanic blocs. These participation phenomena were not noted prior to 1945. Seven of these cities (of a total of eight) are central cities in metropolitan areas. My data also show that while politicians tend less to be the sole figures dominating politics, it is rare today to find a city where their control is totally absent. Also, in earlier decades it was possible to find more towns that were run totally by informal processes. One can conclude that an overall tendency in local communities is away from exclusive leadership by one segment of the population toward combinations, coalitions, and contention of leadership types.

4.

Community power students have recognized the need for cross-national comparisons of communities. Theory, however, had relied upon research in the United States for its substance. Almost ten years ago, when this study was in the first stages of conceptualization, I limited the analysis to communities in the United States in order to control for national differences. At that time I had no real idea what these differences were. Although population size, city type, and economic function are all related to dependent variables of power structures for United States communities, their use for cities of other nations is restricted. They are only useful for those communities located in nations which resemble the United States. Five years ago I tried to suppose on what dimensions the United States might vary from other nation-states in ways that would make a difference for community power analysis among nations. I further supposed that the United States was a deviant case: no other country had the same combination of national features. There appeared to be two features, societal scale[11] and national political ideology.

From a scale and ideology I developed a typology. I drew inferences about what variables should be relevant for local politics in various national structures in this typology. These will be presented, but first I want to say that in the intervening years, I have seen no research from abroad which contradicts these ideas.

Societal Scale

Scale here refers to the extent of territorial interdependence of people and their activities in society. In the pre-industrial city, all social and occupational types are found within the city walls and interdependence among cities is relatively slight. In small-scale societies, there is relatively little differentiation of cities, and educating, food-gathering, cloth-making, tool-making, and servicing will be carried on regardless of population size.

In the United States, it is commonplace to find populations differentiated by age, income, ethnicity, and so on, located in legally autonomous suburbs outside the municipal boundaries of cities. The suburb and city nevertheless are linked in a myriad of ways and they are dependent on a national and international network for raw materials, exports, and so on.

As societal scale increases, people pile up in cities. Centers of communication and coordination locate in specialized areas, and spans of organizational control grow. Some centers supply raw

11. Societal scale is theoretically developed in Eshref Shevky and Wendell Bell, *Social Area Analysis*, and empirically developed in Greer et al., *The New Urbanization*.

materials or food; others process or distribute them. Others per-form all of these activities and are also centers of banking and finance, mass communications, education, or other economic specialties.

The significance of city size and type in the hypotheses, in this and in other American community power studies, is due to the fact that such cities are located within a very large scale society.

TABLE 3–3. SOCIETAL SCALE AND NATIONAL POLITICAL IDEOLOGY ARE BACKGROUND FACTORS FOR COMMUNITY POWER STRUCTURE THEORY

Type	Societal scale	National political ideology	Independent variables for community power theory
1.	Large (Economic function of cities is more variable in 1 and 2 than in 3 and 4.)	Centralized	Population size and city type predict moderately. Formal government is an important predictor.
2.	Large	Decentralized	Theory based upon population size, city type, and economic function predicts best. Formal government has more error as a predictor than in Type 1 and is a weak predictor.
3.	Small (Economic function of cities is less variable in 3 and 4 than 1 and 2.)	Centralized	Population size and city type do not predict — Formal government is a good predictor.
4.	Small	Decentralized	Local norms (existing principals of organization, e.g., clan) are important for prediction.

Size or type of city would not make a difference for local political variations unless other conditions existed. For example, prior to modern times, densely populated China was organized primarily upon the principle of patriarchal clan. Dynasties had relatively little effect on localities because the clans performed the functions of local government.

As a variable, economic function is probably different in char-acter than population size or city type. The existence of both highly diversified cities and wide-ranging functional types indicates that the containing society is large in scale. Scale is small where specialized economic centers are few, and are poorly tied into the social organization of the society. They serve limited geographical areas.

Where economic functional differentiation (scale) is great within a society, size and city type make a difference for local power structures. Where scale is small, population size does not have consequences for community power structures (such as in Egypt or Cambodia). Hypotheses are that a large-scale social organization is a necessary condition (1) for cities to be highly differentiated by economic function and (2) for population size and city type to have consequences for power structures.

National Political Ideology

The political ideology of a nation with regard to belief or acceptance of centralized decision-making must be considered in current theory. An ideology differing from that of the United States exists in other large-scale nations. The United States emphasizes citizen participation and de-emphasizes social planning. The ideology has consequences for local governing. Central planning by government is more acceptable to people in other large-scale nations. Thus, formal authorities are expected to take care of political functions. For example, the future urban growth and development of territory of the Toronto hinterlands is being planned officially. There is no comparable authority in areas of the United States to correspond with that of Canada. In the United States, we do have water-shed districts which transcend municipal and state boundaries, but no authority so strong as to control urban development. In European democracies, there is predictably less citizen participation in planning than in the United States. In dictatorships or totalitarian systems, planning is further centralized. Because of the high degree of centralization in the latter, there is less variety in their local political processes (within any single nation) than in westernized nondictatorships.

Scale and Ideology

Hypotheses based upon the variety of variables presented in the inventory are limited in their generality because of differences among nations in their scale. The independent variables are further limited for use in power structure hypotheses because of the pow-

:rful effect of national political ideology on local processes. Table 3–3 provides a summary for the variables discussed.

The United States is considered "large scale, decentralized," Type 2 in the table. It may be interpreted as follows: "For the American cities currently analyzed, population size, city type, and other variables and attributes already presented, make a difference for power structures. Economic functional variety among cities exists and does so as part of a larger system. The system is ideologically decentralized which allows a de facto variety in local policy-making."

Hypotheses that are supported by data from cities of the United States will probably not be as strongly supported by data from cities of Type 1, such as other Western democracies. Their ideologies favor more centralization and are more socialistic. And, of course, the hypotheses ought to receive even less support (or no support) in totalitarian dictatorships. Formal governmental arrangements and decision-making processes are more concurrent than in the United States.

In the small-scale nations, population size and city type will have even less impact on community power structure features. If the small-scale nation is centralized, Type 3, the formal governmental structure is a good indicator of actual decision-making and enforcing processes. If the ideology favors decentralization, Type 4, the best hypotheses will be based upon the social organization concepts used by anthropologists—the family, clan, patrilineage, tribe, and so forth. These concepts will predict persons who are responsible for the functions of local government and decision-making.

Cities, of course, are involved in national and international processes and these factors ought not to be ignored. Cities can no longer be regarded as independent units of analysis if valid knowledge of local politics is desired.

The propositional inventory was developed to deal with the plethora of generalizations that have developed since the late 1950s about decision-making in the local community. It was both developed and tested with data. I hope that the inventory has helped further the building of empirically based theory and that it has somewhat narrowed the range of acceptable views in the investigated area.

UNIVERSITY OF FLORIDA MONOGRAPHS

Social Sciences

The Whigs of Florida, 1845–1854, y Herbert J. Doherty, Jr.

Austrian Catholics and the Social Question, 1918–1933, by Alfred Diaant

The Siege of St. Augustine in 1702, y Charles W. Arnade

New Light on Early and Medieval apanese Historiography, by John A. Iarrison

The Swiss Press and Foreign Affairs in World War II, by Frederick I. Hartmann

The American Militia: Decade of Decision, 1789–1800, by John K. Maon

The Foundation of Jacques Mariain's Political Philosophy, by Hwa ol Jung

Latin American Population Studes, by T. Lynn Smith

. Jacksonian Democracy on the lorida Frontier, by Arthur W. Thompson

0. Holman Versus Hughes: Extenion of Australian Commonwealth owers, by Conrad Joyner

1. Welfare Economics and Subsidy Programs, by Milton Z. Kafoglis

2. Tribune of the Slavophiles: Kontantin Aksakov, by Edward Chmieewski

3. City Managers in Politics: An Analysis of Manager Tenure and Termination, by Gladys M. Kammerer, Charles D. Farris, John M. DeGrove, and Alfred B. Clubok

14. Recent Southern Economic Development as Revealed by the Changing Structure of Employment, by Edgar S. Dunn, Jr.

15. Sea Power and Chilean Independence, by Donald E. Worcester

16. The Sherman Antitrust Act and Foreign Trade, by Andre Simmons

17. The Origins of Hamilton's Fiscal Policies, by Donald F. Swanson

18. Criminal Asylum in Anglo-Saxon Law, by Charles H. Riggs, Jr.

19. Colonia Barón Hirsch, A Jewish Agricultural Colony in Argentina, by Morton D. Winsberg

20. Time Deposits in Present-Day Commercial Banking, by Lawrence L. Crum

21. The Eastern Greenland Case in Historical Perspective, by Oscar Svarlien

22. Jacksonian Democracy and the Historians, by Alfred A. Cave

23. The Rise of the American Chemistry Profession, 1850–1900, by Edward H. Beardsley

24. Aymara Communities and the Bolivian Agrarian Reform, by William E. Carter

25. Conservatives in the Progressive Era: The Taft Republicans of 1912, by Norman M. Wilensky

26. *The Anglo-Norwegian Fisheries Case of 1951 and the Changing Law of the Territorial Sea*, by Teruo Kobayashi

27. *The Liquidity Structure of Firms and Monetary Economics*, by William J. Frazer, Jr.

28. *Russo-Persian Commercial Relations, 1828–1914*, by Marvin L. Entner

29. *The Imperial Policy of Sir Robert Borden*, by Harold A. Wilson

30. *The Association of Income and Educational Achievement*, by Roy L. Lassiter, Jr.

31. *Relation of the People to the Land in Southern Iraq*, by Fuad Baali

32. *The Price Theory of Value in Public Finance*, by Donald R. Escarraz

33. *The Process of Rural Development in Latin America*, by T. Lynn Smith

34. *To Be or Not to Be . . . Existential-Psychological Perspectives on the Self*, edited by Sidney M. Jourard

35. *Politics in a Mexican Community*, by Lawrence S. Graham

36. *A Two-Sector Model of Economic Growth with Technologic. Progress*, by Frederick Owen Goddard

37. *Florida Studies in the Helping Professions*, by Arthur W. Combs

38. *The Ancient Synagogues of th Iberian Peninsula*, by Don A. Halperin

39. *An Estimate of Personal Wealth in Oklahoma in 1960*, by Richard Edward French

40. *Congressional Oversight of Executive Agencies*, by Thomas A. Henderson

41. *Historians and Meiji Statesmen* by Richard T. Chang

42. *Welfare Economics and Peak Load Pricing: A Theoretical Application to Municipal Water Utility Practices*, by Robert Lee Greene

43. *Factor Analysis in International Relations: Interpretation, Problem Areas, and an Application*, by Jack E. Vincent

44. *The Sorcerer's Apprentice: The French Scientist's Image of German Science, 1840–1919*, by Harry W. Paul

45. *Community Power Structure: Propositional Inventory, Tests, and Theory*, by Claire W. Gilbert

UNIVERSITY OF FLORIDA PRE
GAINESVILLE
1972